A SHORT GUIDE TO RISK APPETITE

SHORT GUIDES TO RISK SERIES

Risk is a far more complex and demanding issue than it was ten years ago. Risk managers may have expertise in the general aspects of risk management and in the specifics that relate directly to their business, but they are much less likely to understand other more specialist risks. Equally, Company Directors may find themselves falling down in their duty to manage risk because they don't have enough knowledge to be able to talk to their risk team in a sensible way.

The short guides to risk are not going to make either of these groups experts in the subject but will give them plenty to get started and in a format and an extent (circa 150 pages) that is readily digested.

Titles in the series will include:

- Climate Risk
- Compliance Risk
- Employee Risk
- Environmental Risk
- Fraud Risk
- Information Risk
- Intellectual Property Risk
- Kidnap and Ransom Risk
- Operational Risk
- Purchasing Risk
- Reputation Risk
- Strategic Risk
- Supply Chain Risk
- Tax Risk
- Terrorism Risk

Visit www.gowerpublishing.com/shortguidestorisk for details of the latest titles, sample chapters and help on requesting a standing order.

A Short Guide to Risk Appetite

David Hillson
and
Ruth Murray-Webster

GOWER

Published by
Gower Publishing Limited
Wey Court East
Union Road
Farnham
Surrey GU9 7PT
England

Gower Publishing Company
Suite 420
101 Cherry Street
Burlington, VT 05401-4405
USA

www.gowerpublishing.com

British Library Cataloguing in Publication Data
Hillson, David, 1955-
  A short guide to risk appetite. -- (Short guides to
  business risk series)
  1. Risk management.
  I. Title II. Series III. Murray-Webster, Ruth.
  658.1'55-dc23

  ISBN: 978-1-4094-4094-9 (pbk)
        978-1-4094-4095-6 (ebk)
        978-1-4094-8463-9 (epub)

Library of Congress Cataloging-in-Publication Data
Hillson, David, 1955-
  A short guide to risk appetite / by David Hillson and Ruth Murray-Webster
Gower.
      p. cm. -- (Short guides to business risk)
  Includes index.
  ISBN 978-1-4094-4094-9 (pbk.) -- ISBN 978-1-4094-4095-6 (ebook)
  1. Risk management. 2. Decision making. I. Murray-Webster, Ruth. II. Title.
  HD61.H4775 2012
  658.15'5--dc23

2012023449

Printed and bound in Great Britain by the
MPG Books Group, UK

Contents

List of Figures

List of Tables

Foreword

I have read David and Ruth's book with great interest and there is lots of value in having a clear summary of this important issue.

The book provides clarity around definitions and as this is an area of real and on-going confusion, this is a major benefit.

The book also provides a really useful framework that the risk professional can use to structure their thinking and to shape their interactions with management.

Shaping appropriate communication, to engage managers across an organisation to consider risk thresholds is a vital activity and the RARA Model builds up a comprehensive picture of the inputs to and influences on risk thresholds, and the controls to ensure that organisations take an *appropriate amount* of risk in pursuing their objectives.

This model can then be used to shape communication that fits the maturity and culture of the organisation and the way the book deals with the three scenarios of increasing maturity in this area is very helpful in informing how my own organisation approaches this, and where we can improve in the future.

Dr Mark Davies, Head of Group Risk, Rio Tinto plc

Preface and Acknowledgements

For the past decade we have shared a mission to 'put people into risk management'. This means going beyond risk management theories, methods, tools and techniques in order to help people at all levels in organisations to see how they can make risk management add tangible value for them. We've captured some of our thinking on this important topic in our previous books *Understanding and Managing Risk Attitude* and *Managing Group Risk Attitude*.

After writing extensively about risk attitude, we continue to find that people confuse risk attitude with risk appetite. A lot of people are now talking about risk appetite since it has become embedded in risk standards and guidance documents. We felt strongly that risk appetite, risk attitude and other risk-related terms need to be understood not separately but in the context of each other. We met to discuss this, and a couple of hours later we'd developed the RARA Model that forms the heart of this book! As with all our work, we're seeking to shed light on important topics, offering practical guidance based on leading-edge insights. We hope that this book meets these aims, and we invite our readers to let us know whether we've succeeded.

We are grateful once again to Jonathan Norman at Gower Publishing who welcomed our proposal to expand the Short

Guide Risk series with this *Short Guide to Risk Appetite*. Jonathan and the Gower team are great to work with and we appreciate their support.

We are also grateful to Mark Davies, Head of Group Risk at Rio Tinto plc for reading the manuscript and writing the Foreword.

Finally, and as always, our long-suffering and ever-loving families Liz, Tess and Mark, Kate and Stu (the Hillsons) and Fred, Josh and Helen (the Murray-Websters) deserve a mention. We believe that the ability to manage risk well is a life skill, not just for the business setting. We've tried to reflect that in our role as parents over the years, with varying degrees of success. But nothing is more important to a young person than answering the 'How much risk ... ?' questions that we address in this book. So as each of our children faces their unique challenges at their different stages of life, we dedicate this book to them with love and hope.

David Hillson and Ruth Murray-Webster

1 Why is Risk Appetite Important?

The world is faced with levels of uncertainty that fundamentally matter if countries, organisations, projects and people are to reach their objectives. Leaders and managers of organisations, from the biggest government to the smallest family unit, have no choice but to make decisions about how to respond to uncertainty all around them. Shall we lend this money – to another country, or to a friend? Shall we borrow this money – from this bank, or from a relative? Shall we indulge ourselves today and decide what to do tomorrow when it comes, or shall we restrain ourselves today and hope we can convince those influenced directly by our 'austerity measures' or 'cuts' that this is in their best interests? Shall we look after our shareholders/ourselves following the old adage 'charity begins at home', or shall we reach out to help our 'neighbours' in the world as much as we can?

These are important questions to get right. If you are too cautious it is likely to be difficult to comply with your some of your values and standards and to achieve your objectives. The opposite is also true – it is likely to be difficult to align with values and standards and reach objectives if you just 'go with your gut' and pursue what you want in the short term. As with so many things in life, we need to find a way of achieving some sort of balance – not a mediocre midpoint, but a way of understanding the trade-offs we are making when we decide on a course of action.

Decision-makers probably only ask themselves these types of question explicitly on an infrequent basis. More routinely they play out their 'strategy' on these topics through a series of day-to-day decisions. That's why strategy is often referred to as a 'pattern of decisions'. If decisions are random, ad hoc or conflicting with earlier decisions, they are unlikely to take the organisation to where it wants to be long term. So establishing a way of making strategically consistent decisions is vital.

One way to achieve this consistency is by establishing control mechanisms. Controls are established by countries, organisations and people, to try to make sure that the decisions they take are not reckless, irresponsible or working against the agreed philosophy, principles or strategy that the decision-maker wants to uphold.

An aspect of control that has recently emerged is referred to as 'risk appetite'. Unfortunately there is currently no accepted definition of this term, as we'll discuss in the next chapter. However, this lack of consensus has not stopped risk appetite from quickly becoming a hot topic, with many conferences, journal articles and discussions about the subject. The media also increasingly talks about risk appetite as it reports on failures that are judged to have been caused by decision-makers failing to understand how much risk they should take in a particular scenario.

Anyone who uses risk management and understands its benefits will recognise that the risk process provides risk-based data to inform decision-making. But an explicit link between risk management and decision-making is not always made in practice. The interest shown in risk appetite by regulatory bodies and others has changed this. It is important that we understand risk appetite if we are to make good decisions in uncertain, important situations.

WHY WRITE THIS BOOK?

If risk appetite is a hot topic with lots already written, why did we decide to write a Short Guide on the subject? We have noticed as we carry out our consulting work with organisations large and small across the world that decision-makers are confused about what risk appetite really means and what they need to do.

For example, at a professional meeting early in 2011, we listened to a speaker from a major consultancy talk about risk appetite and give the company's sales pitch to the audience. Throughout the 15-minute talk, the presenter constantly switched between talking about risk appetite and risk attitude, completely mixing up these two things that we believe are significantly different. In a consulting assignment in mid 2011 we were working with senior decision-makers in a major company who want to manage risk responsibly and creatively to deliver value to shareholders and wider society. We discovered that they could not engage with the current definitions of risk appetite as published and they didn't know how to apply the concept sensibly. We talked, and this book was born.

3

WHO IS THIS BOOK FOR?

This book is written for decision-makers in a whole range of organisations.

Certainly it is for senior managers and directors responsible for corporate governance, investment decisions and the social responsibility agenda in their organisation, and it applies equally to public, private and 'third' or charitable sectors of all sizes.

Many organisations have risk professionals to help them navigate the complexities of making decisions in risky and important situations, and this book is equally written for risk managers, risk practitioners, risk advisers, risk analysts, risk facilitators and risk champions (or any other risk-related role).

It will also be of interest to HR professionals and others interested in organisational or behavioural psychology who need to know how to influence organisational outcomes.

Students, researchers and practitioners interested in decision-making under uncertainty will also find that we cover the topic from a wide-ranging perspective – although the book is written as practical guide for decision-makers rather than as an academic text.

We write for an international audience, since the principles are generic and apply to all situations and industries where people are managing risk. Although we often work in supporting managed change through programmes and projects, the principles in the book are equally applicable to making risk management work at strategic or operational levels as well as in project/change-based settings. The subject matter of this book should be particularly attractive to people working in business or public service in countries facing the economic challenges arising from the global financial crisis, where the imperative to be seen to be managing risk responsibly is critical at this time.

Finally, we write in the hope that people who use our ideas in their work situation will also think about how it might apply to their family or the social organisations they interact with, such as local churches, sports clubs, musical societies and so on.

WHAT PRIOR KNOWLEDGE ARE WE ASSUMING?

We assume no prior knowledge of risk appetite or any other risk-related terms other than a basic knowledge of the part risk management plays in an organisation. For those who are thinking about risk management for the first time, we'd recommend that you read some of our other work, for example *Exploiting Future Uncertainty: Creating Value from Risk* (Hillson, 2010) or *A Short Guide to Facilitating Risk Management: Engaging Others to Identify, Own and Manage Risk* (Pullan and Murray-Webster, 2011). We expect it may be easier for people with no knowledge of risk appetite to engage with the ideas in our book as they will not have been influenced by other texts. We recognise, though, that most of our readers will be interested in the subject because they have heard about and thought about risk appetite before and want to find out more about the subject. Recognising this, Chapter 2 provides a detailed summary of the risk appetite 'story so far', referencing specifically what regulators, standards bodies, professional associations and consultants have already published. You'll find there isn't much agreement. We take the topic, dissect it, then put it back together in a way that is intended to be totally practical and implementable in a variety of situations.

WHAT COMES NEXT?

Chapter 2 grounds this Short Guide in the context of the story so far and shows where the problems arise. One immediately obvious problem is confusion between risk appetite and other risk-related terms, especially risk attitude. To address this problem, in Chapter 3 we explore the roots of the two concepts to help us understand what risk appetite is and isn't. In the light of the current terminology war, we aim to bring the conflict to a peaceful and stable conclusion.

Chapter 4 extends the argument to build a full taxonomy of risk-related terms and a holistic model that shows how they all relate when making risky and important decisions. We call this the Risk Appetite-Risk Attitude Model, or RARA Model and in Chapter 5 we build four worked examples to show how to apply the model in three stages. We start where decision-making is unmanaged, without an understanding of 'how much risk is too much risk'. The next step is where decision-makers are knowingly constrained by risk appetite but they don't know how to act if they find that they need to overcome this restriction. Finally we show how to move to an informed approach that takes full account of all relevant factors and produces an optimal outcome.

Because risk appetite as an idea is fundamentally linked to matters of decision-making and controls, Chapter 6 picks up the theme of measurement, exploring what can be measured, rationally and objectively, and what can't. Establishing measures is crucial to success, so we aim to provide clarity about what is useful to measure and where it would be futile to try.

Chapter 7 then takes the RARA Model, our insights on measurement from Chapter 6, and the three scenarios of unmanaged, constrained and informed decision-making from Chapter 5 and suggest a simple step-wise process for determining the appropriate amount of risk to take in a situation. We show how you can apply the ideas in practice to inform your decision-making in risky and important situations. In this way you'll be best able to protect your objectives from the threats posed by today's challenges, as well as taking advantage of the myriad opportunities offered by uncertainty.

The final Chapter 8 provides the business case for applying the RARA Model in practice. It reiterates that the current confusion between terms and practice is damaging our society and economy, and that sorting out how to determine 'how much risk should we take' is a vital decision-making capability.

SUMMARY

We believe that it is important for people who are charged with making decisions on behalf of others to do the best they can to safeguard the world, its resources and its impact on the current and future generations.

All decisions are made in the face of risk – uncertainties that would matter to objectives if they occurred.

We argue that it's impossible to make good decisions in risky and important situations if you haven't considered how much risk would be too much risk to take in the situation, and if you've not put in place mechanisms and controls to ensure that you stay on track as time passes. Our aim through this book is help people know how to do this – in practice, not just in principle.

REFERENCES

Hillson D. A. 2010. *Exploiting Future Uncertainty: Creating Value From Risk*. Farnham, UK: Gower.

Pullan P. and Murray-Webster R. 2011. *A Short Guide To Facilitating Risk Management: Engaging People To Identify, Own and Manage Risk*. Farnham, UK: Gower.

② The Risk Appetite Story So Far

We've seen in Chapter 1 that decision-makers at all levels need to understand their own risk appetite as well as the risk appetite of other stakeholders. Without that understanding it's not possible to make appropriate decisions about how much risk to take. That's why risk appetite has become a hot topic recently. It seems everyone is talking about it, thinking about it, writing about it. This chapter summarises what they're saying, to give a sense of the current debate and state of play. Unfortunately, as we'll see, there's not a lot of agreement.

So who is currently talking about risk appetite? We've identified four groups of people:

1. Regulators

2. Standards bodies

3. Professional associations

4. Consultants.

Let's see what they have to say on the subject.

REGULATORS

Across the globe, corporate governance regulators have woken up to the importance of risk appetite. Recent guidelines from some of the most important regulators now refer to the need for organisations to define and communicate their risk appetite, although they don't always use that term explicitly. Many boards of major organisations have recognised that they need to comply with these guidelines, so they have tried to express their risk appetite in corporate policies or annual reports. Unfortunately, without knowing precisely what is required, it's hard for senior executives to know whether they are actually complying or not.

The problem arises because the various regulatory bodies do not use consistent terms. We can illustrate this by looking at corporate governance guidelines from the USA, South Africa, Australia, UK and Europe.

- In the USA, the National Association of Corporate Directors (NACD) Blue Ribbon Commission issued their 'Report on Risk Governance: Balancing Risk and Reward' in October 2009. This states that 'The Board of Directors need to understand the organization's risk appetite and level of risk tolerance. The assessment of the company's risk appetite should be an ongoing process, considering that risks facing the company are constantly changing.' Setting risk appetite is described as 'a strategic decision' for which directors are responsible. Elsewhere the report says that directors need to agree on 'the appropriate level of risk that is acceptable given the company's strategy – the risk appetite'. The report summary says 'An important role for the board is to understand and agree on the company's risk appetite – or the level of risk – that their organization is willing to accept in order to meet its strategic objectives.'

- Also in 2009 the American Committee of Sponsoring Organizations of the Treadway Commission (known as COSO), issued guidelines on Enterprise Risk Management which included a definition of risk appetite as 'the amount of risk, on a broad level, an organization is willing to accept in pursuit of stakeholder value'. The terminology used is similar to NACD, although the goal is generating stakeholder value rather than meeting strategic objectives. These guidelines were significantly expanded in 2012, explaining how risk appetite relates to risk tolerance, and how risk appetite should be understood and communicated.

- In September 2009 the Institute of Directors in Southern Africa issued the third edition of the 'King Report on Governance for South Africa' (King III). This mentions risk appetite in Principle 4.2, which says that 'The board should determine the level of risk tolerance: The board should set the levels of risk tolerance once a year. The board may set limits for the risk appetite. The board should monitor that risks taken are within the tolerance and appetite levels.' King III defines risk appetite as 'The level of residual risk that the company is prepared or willing to accept without further mitigation action being put in place, or the amount of risk the company is willing to accept in pursuit of value.' (Unfortunately it does not define risk tolerance.)

- In 2007, the Australian Securities Exchange (ASX) Corporate Governance Council issued a second edition of their

'Corporate Governance Principles and Recommendations', in which Principle 7 covers the need to 'Recognise and manage risk'. An accompanying guide published in June 2009 describes how to meet this principle, starting with the advice to 'Understand your company's overall risk tolerance'. The guide goes on to say that 'Risk tolerance is the amount of total risk that a company is prepared to accept or be exposed to at any point in time. It can be viewed in one sense as the organisation's attitude towards risk management.'

- In the UK, a revised Corporate Governance Code was issued by the Financial Reporting Council (FRC) in June 2010. Although the specific term 'risk appetite' is not used in the final document, the code states that: 'The board is responsible for determining the nature and extent of the significant risks it is willing to take in achieving its strategic objectives'. An early draft of the revised code did talk about 'defining the company's risk appetite and tolerance', but during the consultation period respondents questioned whether the terminology that the FRC had used properly conveyed the intention behind the new principle. The FRC reported that 'a number of respondents were concerned that the terms risk appetite and risk tolerance were not well understood or that there was no common agreement on their meaning. Others pointed out that, within financial sectors, they tended to be associated with specific metrics and modelling techniques, and were concerned that these might be imposed on companies in other sectors for which they were not suitable.'

- Most recently, in April 2011 the European Commission issued a Green Paper for consultation, called 'The

EU Corporate Governance Framework' (Report COM[2011]164). This seeks to strengthen the corporate governance requirements for European companies, and it mentions the topic of risk appetite. For example the EC Green Paper says 'To be effective and consistent any risk policy needs to be clearly "set from the top" that is, decided by the board of directors for the whole organization. It is generally recognised that the board of directors bears primary responsibility for defining the risk profile of a given organization according to the strategy followed and monitoring it adequately to ensure it works effectively.' In the same section they go on to ask this question: 'Do you agree that the board should approve and take responsibility for the company's "risk appetite" and report it meaningfully to shareholders?' In their response to the EC Green Paper, the Federation of European Risk Management Associations (FERMA) provided a specific answer to this question. Their official statement to the EC stated 'FERMA agrees with the Commission's view that the board plays a key role in setting an organization's risk appetite and monitoring senior management's response to risk. ... FERMA does not necessarily agree that explicit disclosure of a company's risk appetite to shareholders is the most appropriate course of action ... FERMA does not support the proposition to disclose more information about risk appetite, because it may harm companies' competitive position, will not improve its risk management culture, and will not provide more assurance to stakeholders that risks are better under control.' This response is interesting as it provides the first sign of resistance to the increasing demand from regulators for companies to define and express their corporate risk appetite. It's currently not clear where this might lead, and whether organisations may start to push back against the tide.

This brief survey of some leading corporate governance guidelines shows how terms are used inconsistently and with overlapping meaning:

- NACD and COSO in the USA both equate risk appetite with an appropriate and acceptable level of risk.

- King III in South Africa mentions risk appetite when discussing how to set risk tolerance, and defines it as the level of acceptable residual risk.

- Australian ASX guidelines use risk tolerance as the main term, and they say that it can be seen as the same as risk attitude.

- The UK Corporate Governance Code dropped the term risk appetite after the consultation period when respondents said it was not well understood.

- A recent EC consultation paper uses risk appetite in the section about defining risk profile, but these proposals are being opposed by European risk associations.

Risk appetite, risk tolerance, risk attitude, risk profile – all these phrases are used in current corporate governance guidelines. But they appear to be describing the same thing. Clearly this lack of agreement among the regulators can only cause confusion.

STANDARDS BODIES

If the regulators are failing to give clear guidance on risk appetite, perhaps we can look to the standards world to provide some clarity. After all, that's what standards are for.

The obvious place to start is the international risk management standard ISO Guide 73:2009 'Risk Management – Vocabulary', which helpfully includes a normative definition of risk appetite as 'amount and type of risk that an organisation is willing to pursue or retain'. But this guide only provides the language to be used in other standards, and it doesn't explain how to use the various concepts.

For more detail on managing risk we need to turn to the main international risk standard ISO 31000:2009 'Risk Management – Principles and Guidance'. Unfortunately this doesn't mention risk appetite at all. And although the British Standard BS 31100:2011 'Risk Management – Code of Practice and Guidance for the Implementation of BS ISO 31000' repeats the ISO Guide 73 definition of risk appetite, the term isn't used anywhere in the main document.

In the same way, ISO IEC 31010:2009 'Risk Management – Risk Assessment Techniques' mentions risk appetite in several places without defining it. This says that risk assessment criteria can be 'based on … organizational risk appetite', and that risk levels used to prioritise risks 'should be aligned with the organization's risk appetite'. But we're not told what it is or how to define it.

So unfortunately, although the latest international standards mention risk appetite in passing, they fail to offer any guidance on how it can be expressed or used.

The position in the UK is slightly better, since the Office of Government Commerce (OGC) issued their revised 'Management of Risk: Guidance for Practitioners' (M_o_R) in 2010. This national government standard explains that organisations need to define both their risk capacity ('the maximum amount of risk an organisation can bear') as well as their risk appetite ('the amount of risk the organisation, or subset of it, is willing to accept'), and comments that 'it is risky for an organisation to have a risk appetite greater than the risk capacity'. However, despite this promising start, the M_o_R guidelines don't say anything about how to express or use risk appetite in practice.

So it seems that we can't look to standards for help if we want to understand risk appetite. They offer us a definition, but not much more.

PROFESSIONAL ASSOCIATIONS

Another source of information on risk appetite is the various professional associations in the risk field. Although their advice doesn't carry the same weight as official standards, practitioners and others often seek the view of professional risk bodies. Many of them have issued advice to their members aiming to clarify the meaning of risk appetite and how it should be used in practice. What do these risk specialists have to say on the topic?

- In June 2009 the UK Association of Insurance and Risk Managers (AIRMIC) published a report on 'Research into the definition and application of the concept of risk appetite'. This useful report explains why it is important to understand an organisation's risk appetite and it sets out the major benefits of having a clear risk appetite statement. The research was based on a definition of risk appetite as 'the amount or type of risk that an organisation is prepared to seek, accept or tolerate' (taken from the first edition of British Standard BS31100:2008 'Risk Management – Code of Practice', now superseded). AIRMIC asked risk managers whether this definition was useful, and concluded that definitions of risk appetite used in practice vary and not all practitioners followed the standard. Unfortunately, this AIRMIC report didn't go on to propose a solution to the definition dilemma, and nothing further appears to have been published by AIRMIC on this topic since then.

- The Institute of Risk Management (IRM) commissioned a major review on risk appetite and risk tolerance in 2010. They published a consultation report in May 2011, and the final report was issued in September 2011. The report concludes that risk appetite is a useful concept but it is not well defined or understood. In its consultation paper IRM decided to follow the risk appetite definition from the first edition of BS31100:2008 'Risk Management – Code of Practice' (now superseded), but this was modified in the final report to 'The amount of risk that an organisation is willing to seek or accept in the pursuit of its long-term objectives'. The IRM report introduces the idea of multiple risk appetites within an organisation, at strategic, tactical and operational levels. It recognises the influence of organisational risk culture and risk management maturity on the way an organisation approaches risk appetite. And it insists that risk appetite can only be useful if it is measurable. As a global risk education institute, IRM aims to develop a consensus on the meaning, measurement and practical use of risk appetite. While their 2011 report is a step in the right direction, IRM concedes that it is not the definitive final word on the subject, and they expect thinking on risk appetite to continue to develop.

- The Institute of Operational Risk (IOR) produces a series of advice notes called 'Operational Risk Sound Practice

Guidance'. In December 2009 they issued guidance on operational risk appetite, which they define as 'the operational risk an organization is prepared to tolerate'. The IOR note says that operational risk appetite can be expressed by 'deciding, for each type of risk, what is acceptable, what is unacceptable, and the parameters of the area between those two, that is, what is tolerable'. Like the IRM guidance, IOR suggest ways of measuring risk appetite, including both qualitative and quantitative measures.

- ALARM, the UK public risk management association, published its 'National Performance Model for Risk Management in the Public Services' in 2009. This describes what good risk management should look like, and provides a comprehensive assessment framework with five maturity levels. The framework mentions risk appetite in several places, although there is no definition of the term. So senior managers are expected to 'set the criteria/arrangements for the organisation's appetite for taking risks' and ensure that 'there is a common risk language which creates shared understanding of the key partnerships' risk appetite'. However, without a clear understanding of what risk appetite means, it's not clear how these expectations can be met.

- The Society of Actuaries also offers a definition of risk appetite in its guidance to candidates for the Certified Enterprise Risk Analyst (CERA) qualification. This includes an ERM Fact Sheet where risk appetite is defined as 'the level of aggregate risk that an organization can undertake and successfully manage over an extended period of time'. This document also quotes the Basel II accords as saying that risk appetite is 'the broad-based amount of risk an organization or other entity is willing to accept in pursuit of its mission or vision'.

- Although it is not a professional risk association, HM Treasury has had a long interest in managing risk, and has published several guidelines for use by UK government departments and suppliers. In November 2006 they issued three guides on risk appetite under the title 'Thinking about Risk'. These recognise that even in 2006 there were many definitions of risk appetite, but 'they all boil down to how much of what sort of risk an organisation is willing to take'. HM Treasury define risk appetite as 'The amount of risk that an organisation is prepared to accept, tolerate, or be exposed to at any point in time', and they emphasise that 'Risk appetite needs to be considered at all levels of the business – from the ministerial view, which may be influenced by the political climate, down through the business from strategic decisions to operational delivery.' This approach was based on HM Treasury's 'The Orange Book: Management of Risk – Principles and Concepts', which was published in October 2004 and contains a whole chapter on risk appetite. Despite its early publication date, this guidance is still relevant and useful, and it appears to have been ahead of its time.

- In addition to these various forms of guidance from the leading professional risk associations, a number of other risk bodies provide glossaries of risk-related terms on their websites, most of which mention risk appetite. Examples include the following:

  - The Business Continuity Institute (BCI) published its 'Dictionary of Business Continuity Management Terms' in January 2011, including risk appetite as

'Total amount of risk that an organisation is prepared to accept, tolerate, or be exposed to at any point in time.' Interestingly, the dictionary also includes a note from the editor that 'the vagueness of the concept of Risk Appetite seriously limits its value in BCM programmes'.

–   The International Risk Management Institute (IRMI) operates largely in the risk and insurance sector. Its online glossary of insurance and risk management terms includes a definition of risk appetite as 'The degree to which an organisation's management is willing to accept the uncertainty of loss for a given risk when it has the option to pay a fixed sum to transfer that risk to an insurer.' Apart from this definition, IRMI provides no specific guidance on risk appetite, although it does reproduce articles by various commentators on the topic.

–   The website of the Institute of Internal Auditors provides a glossary that defines risk appetite as 'The level of risk that an organisation is willing to accept', and mentions the term in several places in its process description. For example, the chief audit executive needs to take account of risk appetite levels set by management for the different activities or parts of the organisation, appropriate risk responses should be selected to align risks with the organisation's risk appetite, and management are required to report events that exceeded the limits of the organisation's risk appetite.

–   For the Global Association of Risk Professionals (GARP), risk appetite is 'the level of risk exposure an investor is willing to assume in exchange for the potential for a profit'. GARP seems to offer no direct advice on how to use risk appetite in practice.

- The Public Risk Management Association (PRIMA) represents public sector risk managers in the US. Its online glossary defines risk appetite as 'the willingness of an entity to accept a specific level of risk in order to operate in a cost-effective manner'. Again no further guidance is provided on the topic.

Professional risk associations clearly recognise the importance of risk appetite as a hot topic, and many of them are trying to give guidance to their members so that they can express risk appetite in a useful way. Unfortunately, as with risk standards, the professional bodies don't agree on what risk appetite is or how it should be used in practice. If we want consensus or unanimity we'll need to look elsewhere.

CONSULTANTS

Perhaps not surprisingly, many of the major consultancy firms have seen a new business opportunity in the current interest in risk appetite. After all, with no clear lead coming from the standards world or risk professional bodies, organisations will be looking for advice and support as they try to meet corporate governance requirements. Let's see what they say:

- One of the first consultancy firms to offer an opinion in the risk appetite debate was Oliver Wyman, whose paper 'What's your risk appetite?' appeared in May 2007. This describes risk appetite as 'the variability in results that an organization and its senior executives are prepared to accept in support of a stated strategy', recognising that the perspectives of all key stakeholders need to be considered. A risk appetite statement should be prepared with both qualitative and quantitative elements, and an acceptable tolerance level is set for each element. This is then used to drive strategic and operational business decisions in order to optimise the risk-return profile, recognising that not all risk-taking is bad. The intention, according to Oliver Wyman, is to link risk appetite to the strategic growth agenda. Their report ends with a challenge to senior management: if you can't articulate your organisation's desired overall risk appetite, then it is time to take action.

- IBM Financial Services produced 'Risk Appetite: A Multifaceted Approach to Risk Management' in April 2008, based on an IBM survey of financial institutions. This aimed to test whether the commonly understood definition of risk appetite was accepted by survey respondents. Unfortunately, the report does not explicitly present this definition! Instead IBM say 'Typically, risk appetite is thought of as equivalent to risk tolerance. A more useful view of risk appetite, however, balances risk hunger against risk aversion and is multifaceted, taking into account several fundamental considerations.' Although there's a lot of useful information in this IBM report, this failure to offer a clear definition of the subject is disappointing at best and confusing at worst.

- The PricewaterhouseCoopers (PwC) report 'Risk Appetite – How Hungry Are You?' was issued in June 2008. This recognised that risk appetite varied with perspective, and different stakeholders would have different risk appetites. It defined risk appetite as 'the quantum of risk that the firm is willing to accept within its overall [risk] capacity'. The report recognised that risk appetite is related to other important risk concepts, namely risk capacity (the maximum risk that the firm can bear) and risk profile (risks that are currently assumed). It also highlighted the link between risk appetite and risk culture, both at the overall organisational level and within a given company. And finally PwC addressed the need to express risk appetite in some measurable way. The report ends by asking senior management whether they have discussed the organisation's risk appetite, if they know how to measure it, and if they understand the risk appetites of key stakeholders.

- Also in June 2008 the Australian partnership of KPMG issued their advisory report on 'Understanding and Articulating Risk Appetite'. This describes risk appetite as 'the amount of risk … that an organisation is willing to take on in pursuit of value … the total impact of risk an organisation is prepared to accept in the pursuit of its strategic objectives'. It also says that risk appetites can vary between and within organisations, and talks about different ways of measuring risk appetite. Finally the KPMG report links risk appetite to corporate strategy and business performance, with a challenge to its readers to get started and do something now!

- A Towers Watson report called 'Risk Appetite: The foundation of Enterprise Risk Management' came out in 2009. This was written following a survey in which over 60 per cent of companies surveyed said their top short-term priority was to define risk appetite and risk tolerances. This was proving hard, because 'rating agencies have yet to provide the templates or terminology that would ensure a robust approach … lack of guidance makes the task of articulating risk appetite especially complex'. In the absence of a common definition, Towers Watson suggests that risk appetite is 'the appropriate exposure to risk [a company] will accept in order to enhance the organisation's value over a given time frame'. They go on to describe risk tolerances as 'the quantitative expression of risk appetite', and suggest ways of linking these to risk limits that control appropriate risk-taking within the business. Despite this advice, a subsequent survey of 164 risk and finance managers by Towers Watson in 2011 found that only 43 per cent had a formal process for determining and communicating their risk appetite, risk tolerance and/or risk limits.

- Most recently, in December 2011 SAS Institute published their report 'The Art of Balancing Risk and Reward: The role of the board in setting, implementing and monitoring risk appetite'. The text states that 'In essence, risk appetite can be defined as the quantity and types of risk that the organization is willing to assume in pursuit of its strategic objectives.' However the Definitions table of this report says 'Risk appetite is the aggregated account of the board's willingness (to allow management) to take risks in the pursuit of strategic objectives.' So it is not clear whether, in the view of SAS, risk appetite is an amount of risk or an expression of willingness to take risk.

The fact that the major consultancy firms are offering guidance on risk appetite confirms its status as a hot topic and something that organisations need to take seriously. But we find little agreement on what risk appetite actually is, although there is some common thinking on how to express risk appetite and use it to shape business strategy and operations. And each of these consultancies ends their advice on risk appetite by offering to help organisations to express and manage it. Clearly they see the current debate about risk appetite as a potentially lucrative source of new business.

AND THE ANSWER IS ...

Corporate governance regulators, risk standards, professional risk bodies and major consultancies have all offered advice and guidance on risk appetite, but there is little consensus on the main points. Despite the growing and continuing interest in the subject of risk appetite, there is still no agreement on its meaning or practical application. Our brief survey of what various people are saying on the subject shows a wide range of different approaches and views. Everyone agrees that risk appetite is important, but no one agrees on what it is. Clearly this needs to be addressed if we want to help decision-makers to decide how much risk to take.

Table 2.1   Definitions of risk appetite

Source	Definition of Risk Appetite
Regulators	
National Association of Corporate Directors (US)	The level of risk that their organization is willing to accept in order to meet its strategic objectives.
Basel II	The broad-based amount of risk an organization or other entity is willing to accept in pursuit of its mission or vision.
COSO (US)	The amount of risk, on a broad level, an organization is willing to accept in pursuit of stakeholder value.
King III (South Africa)	The level of residual risk that the company is prepared or willing to accept without further mitigation action being put in place, or the amount of risk the company is willing to accept in pursuit of value.
European Commission	The risk profile of a given organization according to the strategy followed.

Table 2.1 **Definitions of risk appetite** *continued*

Source	Definition of Risk Appetite
Standards	
ISO Guide 73:2009	Amount and type of risk that an organization is willing to pursue or retain.
OGC M_o_R	The amount of risk the organisation, or subset of it, is willing to accept.
Professional associations	
Association of Insurance and Risk Managers (AIRMIC)	The amount or type of risk that an organisation is prepared to seek, accept or tolerate.
Business Continuity Institute (BCI)	Total amount of risk that an organisation is prepared to accept, tolerate or be exposed to at any point in time.
Global Association of Risk Professionals (GARP)	The level of risk exposure an investor is willing to assume in exchange for the potential for a profit.
HM Treasury	The amount of risk that an organisation is prepared to accept, tolerate or be exposed to at any point in time.
Institute of Internal Auditors (IIA)	The level of risk that an organisation is willing to accept.
Institute of Operational Risk (IOR)	The [operational] risk an organization is prepared to tolerate.
Institute of Risk Management (IRM)	The amount of risk that an organisation is willing to seek or accept in the pursuit of its long-term objectives.
International Risk Management Institute (IRMI)	The degree to which an organisation's management is willing to accept the uncertainty of loss for a given risk when it has the option to pay a fixed sum to transfer that risk to an insurer.
Public Risk Management Association (PRIMA)	The willingness of an entity to accept a specific level of risk in order to operate in a cost-effective manner.

Table 2.1   Definitions of risk appetite *concluded*

Source	Definition of Risk Appetite
Society of Actuaries	The level of aggregate risk that an organization can undertake and successfully manage over an extended period of time.
Consultants	
Oliver Wyman	The variability in results that an organization and its senior executives are prepared to accept in support of a stated strategy.
IBM	Risk appetite is ... equivalent to risk tolerance ... balances risk hunger against risk aversion and is multifaceted, taking into account several fundamental considerations.
PricewaterhouseCoopers	The quantum of risk that the firm is willing to accept within its overall [risk] capacity.
KPMG	The amount of risk ... that an organization is willing to take on in pursuit of value ... the total impact of risk an organization is prepared to accept in the pursuit of its strategic objectives.
SAS Institute	The quantity and types of risk that the organization is willing to assume in pursuit of its strategic objectives ... the aggregated account of the board's willingness (to allow management) to take risks in the pursuit of strategic objectives.
Towers Watson	The appropriate exposure to risk [a company] will accept in order to enhance the organisation's value over a given time frame.

Table 2.1 draws together all the definitions we have discussed in this chapter. Looking at the range of definitions, we can see a huge variation in the specific words used, but two general themes emerge:

1. Firstly, many of these definitions say that risk appetite is a 'level, amount or quantum of risk'. In other words, risk appetite is expressed in the same terms as risk itself, and presumably can be quantified using the same units as risk.

2. But secondly, risk appetite is also described in terms of the level of risk that an organisation is willing or prepared to accept/pursue/retain/seek/tolerate/assume/take on be exposed to. This is more about how an organisation approaches risk, and is perhaps more difficult to express: what units do we use to measure 'willingness'?

We will return to these two themes in the next chapter, as they point to an important distinction in how we should understand and approach risk appetite. Clearly risk appetite is something to do with an amount of risk, and it is appropriate and possible to ask 'How much?' But there is also clearly an aspect of the risk appetite discussion that is about our response to that perceived risk exposure, where the question is more like 'So what?'

One other thing emerges from our examination of the way risk appetite is used by others. Delving more deeply into the way these various sources describe risk appetite, we find that it is often explained by using other risk-related terms, for example saying that risk appetite is 'a threshold' or 'an attitude' or 'a tolerance'.

This loose use of terms is really unhelpful. In fact a wider review of what others have written on risk appetite reveals a whole host of other words that are used interchangeably with risk appetite. These include risk attitude, risk capacity, risk culture, risk exposure, risk perception, risk preference, risk profile, risk propensity, risk threshold, risk tolerance (and others). No one seems able to define how these terms might differ, overlap, replace or relate to each other.

Before we can move on to consider how to express risk appetite, we need to dispel the confusion by providing a clear definition of what it is, and we also need to distinguish it from other related risk terms. The next chapter addresses this challenge.

REFERENCES

ALARM. 2009. *National Performance Model for Risk Management in the Public Services*. Available at: http://www. alarm-uk.org/PDF/Alarm%20National%20Performance%20 Model.pdf. Accessed 18 August 2012.

Association of Insurance and Risk Managers. 2009. *Research into the Definition and Application of the Concept of Risk Appetite*. London, UK: Association of Insurance and Risk Managers.

Australian Securities Exchange (ASX) Corporate Governance Council. 2007. *Corporate Governance Principles and Recommendations* (second edition). Available at: http://asx. ice4.interactiveinvestor.com.au/ASX0701/Corporate%20 Governance%20Principles/EN/body.aspx?z=1&p=-1&v=1&uid=. Accessed 18 August 2012.

Australian Securities Exchange (ASX) Markets Supervision. 2009. Principle 7: Recognise and Manage Risk: Guide for small-mid market capitalised companies. Available at: http://www.asx.com.au/documents/about/final_principal_7_deloitte_blakiston_crabb_2009.pdf. Accessed 18 August 2012.

British Standard BS 31100:2008. 2008. *Risk Management – Code of Practice*. London, UK: British Standards Institution.

British Standard BS 31100:2011. 2011. *Risk Management – Code of Practice and Guidance for the Implementation of BS ISO 31000*. London, UK: British Standards Institution.

Business Continuity Institute (BCI). 2011. *Dictionary of Business Continuity Management Terms*. Available at: http://www.thebci.org/Glossary.pdf. Accessed 18 August 2012.

Committee of Sponsoring Organizations of the Treadway Commission (COSO). 2004. *Enterprise Risk Management – Integrated Framework*. New York NY, USA: AICPA.

Committee of Sponsoring Organizations of the Treadway Commission (COSO). 2009. *Effective Enterprise Risk Oversight: The Role of the Board of Directors*. Available at http://www.coso.org/documents/COSOBoardsERM4pager-finalreleaseversion82409_001.pdf. Accessed 18 August 2012.

Committee of Sponsoring Organizations of the Treadway Commission (COSO). 2012. *Enterprise Risk Management – Understanding and Communicating Risk Appetite*. Available at http://www.coso.org/documents/ERM-Understanding%20%20Communicating%20Risk%20Appetite-WEB_FINAL_r9.pdf. Accessed 18 August 2012.

European Commission. 2011. *The EU Corporate Governance Framework* (Report COM[2011]164). Available at: http://ec.europa.eu/internal_market/company/docs/modern/com2011-164_en.pdf. Accessed 30 August 2011.

Federation of European Risk Management Associations (FERMA). 2011. Response to EC Green Paper. Available at: http://www.ferma.eu/Portals/2/documents/european%20affairs/FERMA_position_on_CG_green_paper_June2011.pdf. Accessed 18 August 2012.

Financial Reporting Council. 2010. *UK Corporate Governance Code*. London, UK: Financial Reporting Council.

Global Association of Risk Professionals (GARP). 2011. *Online Glossary*. Available at: http://www.garp.org/risk-news-and-resources/risk-glossary/risk-glossary.aspx. Accessed 18 August 2012.

HM Treasury. 2004. *The Orange Book: Management of Risk – Principles and Concepts*. Available at: http://www.hm-treasury.gov.uk/d/orange_book.pdf. Accessed 18 August 2012.

HM Treasury. 2006. *Thinking about Risk. Managing Your Risk Appetite – A Practitioner's Guide*. Available at: http://www.hm-treasury.gov.uk/d/tar_practitioners_guide.pdf. Accessed 18 August 2012.

HM Treasury. 2006. *Thinking about Risk. Managing Your Risk Appetite – Good Practice Examples*. Available at: http://www.hm-treasury.gov.uk/d/tar_goodpractice_examples.pdf. Accessed 18 August 2012.

HM Treasury. 2006. *Thinking about Risk. Setting and Communicating Your Risk Appetite*. Available at: http://www.hm-treasury.gov.uk/d/tar_riskappetite.pdf. Accessed 18 August 2012.

IBM Financial Services. 2008. *Risk Appetite: A Multifaceted Approach to Risk Management*. Armonk NY, USA: IBM.

Institute of Directors in Southern Africa. 2009. *King Report on Governance for South Africa* (3rd edition, King III). Available at: http://www.iodsa.co.za/Portals/0/IoDSA_King_Code_Flip_Book/IoDSA_King_Code_Flip_Book.html. Accessed 18 August 2012.

Institute of Internal Auditors. 2011. *Online Glossary*. Available at: http://www.theiia.org/guidance/standards-and-guidance/ippf/standards/full-standards/?i=8317. Accessed 18 August 2012.

Institute of Operational Risk. 2009. *Operational Risk Sound Practice Guidance Part 1: Risk Appetite* (version 1, December 2009). Available at: http://www.ior-institute.org/education/sound-practice-guidance/8-sound-practice-guidance-part-1. Accessed 30 August 2011.

Institute of Risk Management. 2011. *Risk Appetite and Tolerance*. London, UK: Institute of Risk Management.

International Organization for Standardization ISO 31000:2009. 2009. *Risk Management – Principles and Guidelines*. Geneva, Switzerland: International Organization for Standardization.

International Organization for Standardization ISO Guide 73:2009. 2009. *Risk Management – Vocabulary.* Geneva, Switzerland: International Organization for Standardization.

International Organization for Standardization ISO IEC 31010:2009. 2009. *Risk Management – Risk Assessment Techniques.* Geneva, Switzerland: International Organization for Standardization.

International Risk Management Institute (IRMI). 2010. *Glossary of Insurance and Risk Management Terms.* Available at: http://www.irmi.com/forms/online/insurance-glossary/terms.aspx. Accessed 18 August 2012.

KPMG. 2008. *Understanding and Articulating Risk Appetite.* Sydney, Australia: KPMG.

National Association of Corporate Directors. 2009. *Report on Risk Governance: Balancing Risk and Reward.* Washington DC, USA: National Association of Corporate Directors.

Oliver Wyman. 2007. *What's Your Risk Appetite?* Available at: http://www.oliverwyman.com/media/Risk_Appetite_CRC_0705.pdf. Accessed 18 August 2012.

PricewaterhouseCoopers. 2008. 'Risk appetite – How hungry are you?' *The PwC Journal*, Special risk management edition. London, UK: PricewaterhouseCoopers.

Public Risk Management Association (PRIMA). 2011. *Risk Management Glossary.* Available at: http://www.primacentral.org/content.cfm?sectionid=133. Accessed 18 August 2012.

SAS Institute Inc. 2011. *The Art of Balancing Risk and Reward: The Role of the Board in Setting, Implementing and Monitoring Risk Appetite.* Cary NC, USA: SAS Institute Inc.

Society of Actuaries. 2011. *Enterprise Risk Management Fact Sheet.* Available at http://www.ceranalyst.org/about-erm. asp. Accessed 18 August 2012.

Towers Perrin. 2009. *Risk Appetite: The Foundation of Enterprise Risk Management.* London, UK: Towers Watson.

Towers Watson. 2011. *2011 Risk and Finance Manager Survey.* London, UK: Towers Watson.

UK Office of Government Commerce. 2010. *Management of Risk: Guidance for Practitioners*, 3rd edition. London, UK: The Stationery Office.

③ Terminology Wars

We've seen in Chapter 2 that many different risk-related terms are used when people try to answer the question 'How much risk should we take?' There seems to be some convergence on 'risk appetite' as the right phrase, with regulators, standards bodies, professional risk associations and consultants all using it. But unfortunately these players use the term in different ways causing real confusion. We think it would be really useful to sort this out and have a consistent and coherent taxonomy of risk-related terms which clarifies how these relate to each other. We'll address the full taxonomy in Chapter 4, but first we need to consider two central terms in this field. Risk appetite is one, of course, and the other is risk attitude.

Why these two? There are several important reasons. Firstly, as we listen to the emerging discussion around risk appetite, we often hear people talking about risk attitude in the same breath. The relationship between these two concepts obviously needs to be clarified, given that the words sound similar and therefore could easily be mistaken. Secondly, it seems to be very common for people to get confused between risk appetite and risk attitude in practice, even when they have some understanding of the concepts. And thirdly, our previous work on risk attitude has resulted in some important insights that are relevant to the risk appetite discussion.

The most important reason though arises from our review in Chapter 2 of the various ways people describe risk appetite. Looking widely across regulators, standards, professional bodies and consultants, we found two common themes emerging repeatedly:

1. They say that risk appetite is something to do with an amount or level of risk.

2. They also say that risk appetite is about willingness to accept or tolerate risk.

We agree that both of these aspects are important when considering how much risk an individual or organisation should take in a given situation. But we think the two elements are different in nature. As we'll see below, the first is outside our control where the second is a personal choice.

We can unravel this distinction by addressing one simple question: what is the difference between risk appetite and risk attitude?

NON-TECHNICAL ORIGINS

The terms risk appetite and risk attitude both have their roots in ordinary words that have everyday meanings. These roots are not accidental, and the common-use definitions give us important clues to what their risk versions mean. Let's look in more detail at the two root words.

WHAT IS APPETITE?

For most people, the word appetite is closely linked with being physically hungry. But dictionary definitions of appetite are wider. Of course they include a desire for food or drink, but appetite can also mean a desire to satisfy some other bodily craving, such as sexual pleasure. There are also non-physical appetites, where the desired result is intangible, such as an appetite for excitement or fame. And some appetites can be destructive, involving drugs or violent behaviour. The word appetite is derived from the Latin word *appetere* which means to desire strongly.

These roots immediately tell us something important about appetite, which most people don't recognise. Appetite is not the same as hunger. Appetite is a desire, a psychological need that demands to be met. The external expression of appetite is hunger, which we experience as a lack of something, and which motivates our behaviour in an attempt to satisfy the internal desire.

One interesting variant on this topic is 'specific appetite', which is the term applied to a drive to eat foods that have particular flavours or contain specific nutrients. Scientists believe that specific appetite is an important part of regulating homeostasis in animals, for example to ensure the correct intake of sodium or calcium. Some suggest that specific appetite controls the amount of calories, vitamins, protein and water that an organism seeks in its diet. It appears that specific appetite in animals is innate, influencing behaviour without conscious choice, and there is speculation that something similar may operate in humans.

So what might influence appetite in a particular individual? There are a wide range of factors, including the following:

- Physical characteristics (size, weight, age, and so on)

- Metabolic rate (high, normal, low)

- State of mind (anxious, calm, stimulated, and so on)

- Underlying state of health (good, poor, diseased)

- Lack of something that is required for good health (nutrients, vitamins, water, and so on)

- Last experience when appetite was satisfied (how long ago, how fully satisfied, and so on).

Several of these influences are outside the immediate control of the individual, at least in the short term, since they arise from one or more inherent characteristics.

Finally in our review of physical appetite, we need to think about how appetite is regulated. This has been the subject of considerable research in recent years, starting with the discovery of the hormone leptin in 1994. The system that regulates appetite has many parts. The hypothalamus in the brain plays a major role, but appetite regulation also involves the gastrointestinal tract, the central and autonomous nervous systems, and a range of hormones. We'll refer back to this complex regulatory system for physical appetite when we make the link to risk appetite later because this biological analogy has a direct link with how we make decisions in risky and important situations.

So we see that appetite is an internal desire or craving for food or some other physical stimulant. It exists within a person, and motivates them to meet a felt need. Appetite is the answer to the question 'How hungry do I feel?' But because physical appetite is intangible and has no units, it is hard to measure or express. It does result in outwardly measurable behaviour, though (eating, for example), and we'll return to this in the next chapter. And although appetite is clearly affected by various other factors (such as metabolism or the time since our last meal), it is not something we can choose or influence as it happens. It just is what it is.

WHAT IS ATTITUDE?

Attitude has two distinct meanings in the dictionary. One definition is about people, where 'attitude' is 'state of mind, mental view or disposition with regard to a fact or state'. But another definition is about the positioning of objects such as aircraft, submarines, spacecraft or missiles, where 'attitude' means 'orientation of axes in relation to some reference plane, usually the horizontal'.

At first sight mental views and aircraft positioning do not seem to have much in common. But if we think of people as pilots of their own attitudinal aircraft, some interesting comparisons emerge:

- The aircraft pilot decides what attitude to adopt in order to position the aircraft to execute the desired manoeuvre. In the same way people can choose a mental attitude that leans them towards a desired response, behaviour or outcome.

- Positioning an aircraft with a particular attitude does not make it move, although it does influence the direction of travel. Some other force is needed to move the aircraft. Similarly the mental attitudes of people need to be combined with motivation if any change is to happen.

- The number of possible attitudes for a moving aircraft is almost unlimited within the three dimensions of space. The same is true for people's mental attitudes, with many possible options that can be chosen in any given situation.

- Extreme attitudes make an aircraft unstable, resulting in loss of control and potentially catastrophic consequences. Similarly a sense of balance is required for individuals and groups if their mental attitudes are not to lead to undesired outcomes.

- A pilot may have a preference for how to position the aircraft, or may usually respond in a particular way by habit. But it is always possible to choose a different attitude if the pilot decides to do so. The same is true for the mental state adopted by people in a given situation – we often react habitually but we could choose differently if we wanted to.

In all of these comparisons, one word appears repeatedly – choice. Attitudes are always *chosen responses* to situations. Some people's attitudes may be deeply rooted and arise from core values or beliefs, where others may be more easily changed. We can always choose which attitude to adopt, although often we just react by habit without intentionally deciding how to respond. But the ability to choose our attitudes is an important part of being human. If our attitudes were fixed then we wouldn't be like aircraft pilots freely flying through the air. Instead we would be like cruise missiles pre-programmed to strike a fixed target, with no responsibility for the outcome and no ability to change.

COMPARING APPETITE WITH ATTITUDE

Now that we've explored the underlying concepts of appetite and attitude, we can start to see some of the important similarities and differences. Let's pick out just one vital way in which they are alike, and one crucial difference, before we move on to look at the risk-related versions.

The one obvious common factor shared by both appetite and attitude is they are internal factors that exist within people. This means that they are invisible to the naked eye. You can't tell for certain just by looking at someone how hungry they are or how they are positioning themselves in relation to a particular situation, although there may be external clues in their behaviour or appearance. This makes appetite and attitude hard to talk about and even harder to measure. It may even be the reason that people confuse the two, since both are invisible.

So appetite and attitude clearly share something in common. But clearly they are not synonyms, and we can't just interchange them freely. The two terms have different meanings, so they must have dissimilar characteristics. We might consider a number of detailed ways in which these two differ, but there is one absolute distinction: attitudes can be chosen but appetite just is what it is. Although both appetite and attitude are influenced by a complex set of other factors, it is hard to intervene consciously to change or control your appetite, whereas changing attitude can be a matter of simple choice.

RISK VERSIONS

So is this relevant to risk management? We firmly believe so. Let's translate this general discussion about appetite and attitude into the risk arena. What does this mean for risk appetite and risk attitude? What can we learn about the way that individuals and organisations decide how much risk to take in a given situation?

Rather unhelpfully, the IRM in its 2011 report on risk appetite chooses to distance itself from the natural metaphor. The report explains that although 'appetite' brings connotations of food, hunger and satisfying one's needs, the specific phrase 'risk appetite' should rather be interpreted in terms of 'fight or flight' responses to perceived risks, and not in terms of 'hunger for risk'. We disagree, and we believe that the appetite metaphor can usefully be applied to the risk arena.

So let's develop definitions of *risk appetite* and *risk attitude*, based on our earlier 'non-risk' definitions of general appetite and attitude.

WHAT IS RISK APPETITE?

Just as natural appetite is an internal desire for something, so risk appetite is something to do with how hungry we are for risk. How much risk do we feel that we can take on in a given situation? Our bodies may have specific cravings for missing nutrients, and risk appetite may also be focused on taking particular types of risk. Our appetite for risk is likely to be influenced by a wide range of other factors, just like our physical appetite, but it exists as an internal drive or desire that is not visible externally. And just as appetite is expressed outwardly through hunger, so risk appetite can be seen in the external decisions we make about how much risk to take. In the physical realm it is useful to separate appetite from hunger, so in the risk world we should make a similar separation, using another term for the external measurable expression of our risk appetite – we suggest either risk tolerance or risk threshold.

Drawing these thoughts together, we define risk appetite as:

Tendency of an individual or group to take risk in a given situation.

WHAT IS RISK ATTITUDE?

We've seen that in general terms attitude is defined as the chosen response or positioning of a person in relation to a reference point. From here it is a simple step to define risk attitude, which describes the position we adopt in relation to a particular risky situation. It is common to speak about only a few specific risk attitudes, such as risk-averse, risk-seeking, risk-tolerant or risk-neutral. But in fact risk attitude exists on a continuous spectrum with an infinite number of possible positions, as illustrated in Figure 3.1. Faced with a given risky situation, a particular individual or group might exhibit a risk attitude anywhere on this spectrum. They might adopt a risk attitude explicitly or their position could be driven by habit, but it is important to remember that a different risk attitude can always be chosen.

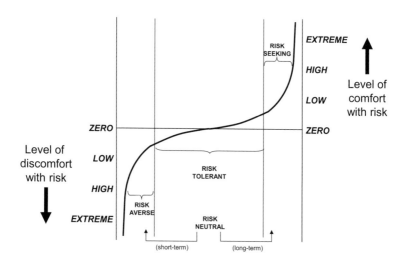

Figure 3.1   **The risk attitude spectrum (from Murray-Webster and Hillson, 2008)**

Of course there are many influences on this choice, including conscious, subconscious and affective factors, as summarised in our 'triple strand' model (Figure 3.2) which we have explained in detail elsewhere (Murray-Webster and Hillson, 2008). While the three parts of the triple strand overlap and interact in complex ways, it is helpful to tease out each of the three elements so that they can be examined and understood.

- **Strand 1 – Conscious factors.** These are the visible and measurable characteristics of a particular risky situation that influence our rational assessment. We also take account of situational factors such as whether we have done anything similar before (familiarity), the degree to which we have control of the situation (manageability), or how soon the situation is expected to affect us (proximity).

CONSCIOUS
FACTORS
(rational
assessments)

SUBCONSCIOUS
FACTORS
(heuristics and
cognitive bias)

... together influence
perception and
risk attitude

AFFECTIVE
FACTORS
(feelings and
emotions)

Figure 3.2   Triple   strand   of   influences   on   risk perception (from   Murray-Webster   and Hillson, 2008)

- **Strand 2 – Subconscious factors.** These include heuristics and other sources of cognitive bias. Heuristics are mental short-cuts based on our previous experience. Some heuristics help us to reach an appropriate position quickly, while others can be misleading. Unfortunately because heuristics are subconscious, their influence is often hidden, and they can be a significant source of bias. Common heuristics include memory of significant events (availability), or the conviction that we already know the right answer (confirmation trap).

- **Strand 3 – Affective factors.** These are gut-level visceral feelings and emotions which tend to rise up automatically or instinctively in a situation and influence how we react. Fear, excitement or attraction can lead us to adopt risk attitudes which a more rational assessment might not consider.

This complex web of influences combines to shape our perception of risk, which in turn affects our choice of risk attitude.

This leads to our definition of risk attitude as:

> *Chosen response to a given risky situation, influenced by risk perception.*

COMPARING RISK APPETITE AND RISK ATTITUDE

Risk appetite and risk attitude are clearly different concepts. And yet we frequently find them confused, even by risk experts and specialists, as Chapter 2 has shown.

There are at least three ways in which risk appetite and risk attitude are alike, and these might help to explain why these two concepts are so often confused:

1. The first and most important similarity is that like their non-risk relatives, both risk appetite and risk attitude are *internal factors*. They exist inside people and can only be seen through some external expression or behaviour. We'll come back to this vital characteristic again later.

2. Another similarity is that risk appetite and risk attitude don't exist in isolation or in a vacuum. They both *only exist in relation to an external situation* which is perceived as both risky and important, and which demands some sort of response. So you have a level of hunger to take risk (or not) in a particular setting, and you then adopt a risk attitude to match the situation. Again we'll see the importance of this later.

3. Lastly, both risk appetite and risk attitude *relate to groups as well as individuals*. It is obvious that each one of us will have a level of risk that we feel comfortable in taking, and that as individuals we can choose what attitude we will adopt in response to our perceived risk exposure. But groups also have risk appetites and risk attitudes. Each project team, management board, family or social club will have a shared view on how much uncertainty they can handle, which we might call their *group risk appetite*. And these same groups can also adopt a common position in how they intend to deal with the risks they face, which is their *group risk attitude*.

But despite these similarities the two concepts are essentially different in nature. The fundamental distinction is that *risk appetite is a tendency* that just is, but *risk attitude is a chosen response*. This difference is crucial in understanding how the two relate, especially when we look at how they operate in a decision-making context.

Both risk appetite and risk attitude play a central role when we have to make decisions in situations that are both risky and important. But their roles are complementary not identical, and they need to work together if we are to make the best possible decisions with good outcomes.

So when we face a risky and important situation and we need to decide how much risk to take, it is inevitable that we will be driven by our internal desire for risk as individuals and/or as an organisation. We could just 'go with our gut' and make an intuitive decision, and of course that might lead to a good outcome. But it might not. This is where risk attitude comes in, allowing us to choose an appropriate positioning towards the risk, modifying our gut reaction if necessary.

These two central steps in the decision-making process form the heart of the matter. There is no doubt that our internal risk appetite will have a strong influence over the way we answer the question 'How much risk *do we want to take* in this situation?' But as intelligent decision-makers we ought also to be sufficiently mature to ask a further question: 'How much risk *should we take*?' The way we answer these two related but different questions will determine how we respond to the risks before us.

It's time to put the various pieces together into a cohesive model that shows the way risk appetite and risk attitude fit into the picture. We'll do that in the next chapter.

REFERENCES

Murray-Webster R. and Hillson D. A. 2008. *Managing Group Risk Attitude*. Aldershot, UK: Gower.

(4) Putting the Pieces Together: The RARA Model

We now know what we mean by two key concepts relating to decision-making in risky and important settings. As a result of Chapter 3 we have the following definitions:

- **Risk appetite** is the tendency of an individual or group to take risk in a given situation.

- **Risk attitude** is the chosen response to a given risky situation, influenced by risk perception.

But we saw in Chapter 2 that many other risk-related terms are used by people when they try to address the question 'How much risk will we take?' It is now time to think about what those other phrases mean, and how they relate to the two central ideas of risk appetite and risk attitude. We'll be considering the following:

- Risk capacity

- Risk culture

- Risk exposure

- Risk perception

- Risk preference

- Risk profile

- Risk propensity

- Risk threshold

- Risk tolerance.

The best way to discover what these mean and how they relate together is to start with the two concepts we already have, and connect them with the others. We'll begin with risk appetite, since this is the main subject of our book.

RISK APPETITE: INPUTS AND OUTCOMES

We've already seen that risk appetite is an internal tendency within an individual or a group, and that it cannot be seen or measured directly. It represents a hunger for risk in a given situation, a desire or drive to take on a certain level of risk exposure. But where does this internal tendency comes from? What influences risk appetite?

In the previous chapter we saw that the system for regulating physical appetite is complex, involving a number of overlapping factors and systems. The same is true for risk appetite, with several influences acting to affect what we eventually experience.

One obvious input to risk appetite is the *situation* that is being faced. Risk appetite does not exist in a vacuum or in isolation. It is defined as 'tendency of an individual or group to take risk *in a given situation*', so clearly that situation is influential. In fact it is not just the situation in general that influences risk appetite, but the specific *objectives* that an individual or organisation wishes to achieve in or from that situation. So for example facing the situation of share price volatility in the stock market, we would expect an organisation deciding whether to float an initial public offering (IPO) to have a different risk appetite from another organisation looking to invest its pension fund. In fact the same organisation would probably exhibit two different risk appetites in relation to those two objectives. Usually objectives are chosen by the individual or group, but sometimes they emerge naturally from the situation. Whatever the path to defining objectives, they need to be well defined and unambiguously expressed if risk appetite is to be determined in a meaningful way.

In addition to the situation and its associated objectives, there are two other factors that influence risk appetite. Both of these are to do with people, which is unsurprising since risk appetite is an internal tendency. The first factor relates to individuals and the other arises from the group context.

- On the individual side, the appetite for risk in a particular situation is affected by the general tendency of each individual to take risk in any circumstances. This is called *risk propensity*, and it in turn is driven by a range of risk-related personality traits, or innate motivations, known as *risk preferences*. Risk-related personality traits can be illustrated by comparing different preferences on commonly available personality diagnostics such as the Myers-Briggs Type Indicator. Using this diagnostic, people with a Perceiving preference like to keep options open and risk-taking, whereas those with a Judging preference favour certainty and firm plans. More on this topic can be found in Chapter 6.

- Another influence on risk appetite is the culture of the group or organisation in relation to risk, describing the set of shared beliefs, values and knowledge that a group has about risk. This is called *risk culture*, and it results in a set of norms and behaviours that are naturally adopted by the group when situations are faced that are perceived as risky and important.

One interesting fact to notice about these inputs to risk appetite is that they are all internal aspects of individuals and groups, and they are not chosen by the individuals separately or the group acting together, they just are what they are. The inputs also each exist before the specific situation arises, and they are not influenced by it. This means that the effect of individual risk propensity and corporate risk culture on risk appetite is subtle and invisible, it is essentially unmanaged, and it cannot be seen or measured externally. The resulting risk appetite therefore arises unconsciously and without the deliberate choice or intentional intervention of the individual or group concerned. That is why we describe risk appetite as a tendency – because it is internal and unmanaged.

We've seen the inputs that affect risk appetite, but we should also consider its outcomes. As discussed in Chapter 3, just as we have no units to measure or describe physical appetite, the same is true for risk appetite. We describe our natural hunger for food or drink by translating the internal appetite into externally measurable terms, for example 'I fancy a steak' or 'I'd just like the salad'. We also need an external proxy for risk appetite, something that can be seen and measured objectively. This role is taken by *risk thresholds*, which are external expressions of risk appetite. And just as risk appetite is defined in terms of the objectives associated with a specific situation, risk thresholds are expressed in the same way. There should be a risk threshold set for each objective, reflecting the overall risk appetite in the situation.

One important feature of risk thresholds is that they can be quantified and measured because they are external and visible – unlike the risk appetite which they express. For example, using the physical analogy of food, our internal appetite may be high or low, but we have no units to describe this directly. Instead we use an amount of food as a proxy, and this can be quantified. So if we fancy a steak, we can then go on to say whether it would take a large T-bone steak weighing 600 grams or 20 ounces to satisfy our appetite, or whether we feel the need to eat a 400-gram/12-ounce sirloin, or maybe we only want a small 150-gram/4-ounce petit-filet. The weight of meat acts as a numerical indicator of our appetite at that specific time and in that particular situation. Risk thresholds are used in exactly the same way to express risk appetite. Each risk threshold relates to a specific objective, and it should be stated as a numerical range that represents upper and lower limits of acceptable uncertainty against that objective, *expressed in the same units as the objective*. Now we have a quantified measure that is externally visible and that stands as a proxy for internal risk appetite. We will return to this in the next chapter.

Once we have defined risk thresholds for a given situation (how much risk we are willing to take), we can then compare these with the overall *risk capacity* of the organisation to bear risk, either in this specific situation or in aggregate. This will tell us whether our risk appetite can be fully satisfied or not.

We might find that our appetite for risk leads us to set risk thresholds that exceed our capacity to take risk. This could lead to a problem if left unmanaged, since we might end up taking on too much risk, for example pursuing a business venture when we are not sure how to fund the cash-flow during development. On the other hand we might find that our risk appetite leads us to be too cautious, setting low risk thresholds which are well within our risk capacity, and which do not stretch or challenge the organisation or make best use of its resources. An example might be an organisation that is not willing to invest in marketing or people development to support growth, preferring instead to retain profits. The problem is that risk appetite and all its inputs are invisible internal factors that are hard to influence directly. This makes it difficult to change things if our risk appetite is leading to inappropriate risk thresholds. We'll come back to this important point later, as clearly some control mechanism is needed if we are to take the right amount of risk in a given situation.

One other risk-related term should be mentioned here before we leave the inputs and outcomes of risk appetite, and that is *risk tolerance*. Risk tolerance has a similar meaning to risk threshold because it is an external expression of risk appetite. Comparing the two directly:

- Risk thresholds are expressed as upper and lower limits around an objective, using the same units of measurement as the objective.

- Risk tolerances describe the permissible degree of accuracy around a value, typically expressed using percentages.

We use the term risk threshold in this book, but the principle underpinning the role of risk thresholds applies equally to risk tolerances.

Let's consider an example. Imagine that we are running a six-month project to upgrade our corporate client management system, with a budget of £100,000. In this situation our organisation or project team will have a tendency to accept some level of risk, which is our risk appetite. We should express this risk appetite by setting risk thresholds against each objective, measured in terms of time, cost and functionality. We could feel a desire to take very little risk with our client database, but feel willing to accept a higher level of cost risk in return. External risk thresholds can then be set against each objective to reflect the internal risk appetite of the organisation in relation to this project. We may decide to set a risk threshold of £80,000 to £120,000 on the budget to define the appetite that exists for pursuing upside risks or accepting downside risks (a risk tolerance of ±20 per cent). However, to reflect a lower appetite for risk with functionality we state that the data error rate must be between 0.01 and 0.02 per cent.

This highlights two key distinctions between risk appetite and risk thresholds/tolerances:

1. Firstly, where risk appetite is *internal* to the individual or group, risk thresholds and tolerances are *externally* expressed. This means that while risk appetite can't be measured, we are able to assign values to risk thresholds and risk tolerances in practice.

2. Secondly, risk appetite is a tendency that arises within people as a result of other influences, but *independent* of

their conscious choice or intervention. Risk thresholds and tolerances on the other hand are *chosen*, decided by the individual or group.

We'll return later to the differences between internal/external and independent/chosen, since these have important implications for how risk appetite can be managed proactively.

So far we've looked at the inputs to and outcomes from risk appetite. In addition to the specific situation and its related objectives, inputs to risk appetite include individual risk propensity, individual risk preferences and organisational risk culture. The main outcome is a set of chosen risk thresholds, expressed in terms of the objectives, possibly with a defined risk tolerance around each threshold. We can define these inputs and outcomes as follows:

- **Risk capacity**: ability of an entity to bear risk, quantified against objectives.

- **Risk culture**: shared beliefs, values and knowledge of a group about risk.

- **Risk preference**: those aspects of an individual's personality and motivation that influence their risk propensity.

- **Risk propensity**: tendency of an individual to take risk in general, informed by inherent risk preferences.

- **Risk thresholds**: quantified measures that represent upper and lower limits of acceptable uncertainty against each objective.

- **Risk tolerance**: the acceptable variance around an objective (an alternative expression of risk thresholds).

The links between these different concepts and risk appetite are shown in Figure 4.1. (Note that risk tolerance is omitted from Figure 4.1 as it is analogous to risk thresholds.)

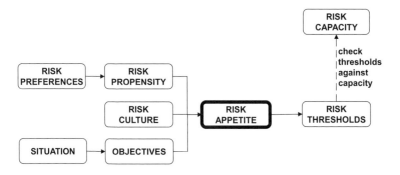

Figure 4.1   Risk appetite inputs and outcomes

RISK ATTITUDE: INPUTS AND OUTCOMES

Now we can turn to the other central concept in this area, risk attitude. What influences the risk attitude of individuals and groups, and what outcomes does it produce?

Risk attitude is the chosen response of an individual or group to a given risky situation, and we have already seen in the previous chapter that it is influenced by *risk perception*. In a decision-making situation, the risk attitude of the people involved in making the decision is affected by their perception of the level of *risk exposure* associated with that situation, and that risk exposure in turn arises from the effect of uncertainty on the objectives.

So the main input to the choice of risk attitude is risk perception. But perception itself is affected by a range of factors, some of which are visible and measurable, while others are hidden within people. We describe these influences as the *triple strand*, including conscious, subconscious and affective factors, as outlined in the previous chapter (see Figure 3.2), and these too form an important input into risk attitude, because they shape our perception of risk. The triple strand is also affected by the particular risky *situation* we are facing. So we consciously assess the level of risk in the situation, but our subconscious biases about that situation influence our perception of risk, and our feelings about the situation also have an effect.

Turning to outputs from risk attitude, two things are important in the context of making decisions in risky and important situations. The first is that our attitude to risk affects the degree of risk we are willing to take, as expressed in *risk thresholds* (also known as risk tolerances, see above). Clearly if we are comfortable with the perceived exposure to risk (that is, our attitude is risk-seeking) then we will wish to set higher risk thresholds than if we are uncomfortable with the uncertainty (risk-averse). But the influence of risk attitude is much wider than simply affecting the chosen level for risk thresholds and tolerances – it also affects our *risk actions*. In fact every action we take in relation to the perceived level of risk exposure is driven by our position on the risk attitude spectrum. Each step in the risk process is affected by the risk attitude we adopt in the situation, including:

- Identifying threats and opportunities

- Assessing and prioritising identified risks

- Selecting and implementing appropriate risk responses.

Our risk actions modify the degree of risk exposure associated with the situation, leading to a revised perception of risk. As a result we may wish to change our risk attitude, to give us the best chance of achieving our objectives in the light of the new risk challenge that we now face. So in fact there should be a cycle between the current level of risk exposure, our chosen risk attitude, and the risk actions we take.

So, having previously described the inputs and outcomes of risk appetite, we have now done the same for risk attitude. In addition to risk thresholds and risk tolerance, which we defined in the preceding section, we can now clarify the definitions of the other risk-related terms that link to risk attitude as follows:

- **Risk actions**. Actions taken to respond to risk exposure, ideally as part of a structured risk process (although this is not always the case).

- **Risk exposure**. A measure of the overall effect of identified risks on objectives. Risk exposure may be expressed quantitatively or qualitatively. *Inherent risk exposure* is the level of risk exposure that exists before risk actions have been implemented. *Residual risk exposure* is the level of risk exposure remaining after agreed risk actions have been implemented.

- **Risk perception**. View of risky situation by individual or group, influenced by the *triple strand*.

- **Triple strand**. Influences on risk perception, formed of conscious, subconscious and affective factors.

These inputs to risk attitude and the outcomes from it are illustrated in Figure 4.2.

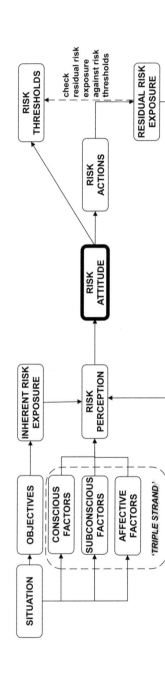

Figure 4.2   Risk attitude inputs and outcomes

When we were discussing risk appetite inputs and outcomes, we noted that all the inputs to risk appetite were internal tendencies that exist within people or groups, and both of the outcomes were external and measurable. We find a similar situation when we look at the factors linked to risk attitude. All of the direct inputs are internal factors with the exception of the initiating situation and the conscious elements of the triple strand, and all of the outcomes are visible externally. We'll discuss the relevance of what can be measured in Chapter 6, but here we'll just point out this interesting similarity between risk appetite and risk attitude. Indeed it is possible that one reason people get confused between risk appetite and risk attitude is the fact that both arise from mostly invisible factors.

PUTTING IT ALL TOGETHER

A close look at Figures 4.1 and 4.2 shows that they have two things in common. Figure 4.1 describes the inputs to risk appetite and the outcomes from it, with one significant input being the specific *situation* that we are facing, whereas the main output is a set of measurable *risk thresholds*. Looking at Figure 4.2, which is about risk attitude, we see the same two items, namely the *situation* as the major input and *risk thresholds* as an outcome. These two common features allow us to link risk appetite with risk attitude, for three reasons:

1. Both risk appetite and risk attitude exist in relation to a specific situation that is perceived as risky and important, and about which we need to make decisions.

2. Both risk appetite and risk attitude are internal factors that are hard to measure, but which have externally visible and measurable outcomes.

3. Both risk appetite and risk attitude affect the risk thresholds that are set in response to a given situation.

Let's see what happens when we put the two figures together into a single integrated model (Figure 4.3). Because this is centred on the two key concepts of risk appetite and risk attitude, we call it the Risk Appetite-Risk Attitude Model, or the RARA Model for short.

As we have already said, one interesting feature of the RARA Model is that some factors are *internal*, existing only within individuals and groups, while others can be seen and measured *externally*. We can also divide the various risk-related factors into those that are under our control and which we can *choose* to modify or manage, and those which exist *independently* of human control. Figure 4.4 classifies the elements of the RARA Model using these two dimensions of internal/external and chosen/independent.

Two important conclusions can be drawn from the classification in Figure 4.4:

1. Only external factors can be seen and measured objectively.

2. Only chosen factors can be changed directly.

It is essential for us to understand these two facts when we consider the way that risk appetite influences decision-making in risky and important situations. This will become clear as we look at how we can manage risk appetite and set risk thresholds in order to answer our key question: 'How much risk will we take in this situation?' The following chapters explore this in detail, but we can outline the main idea here.

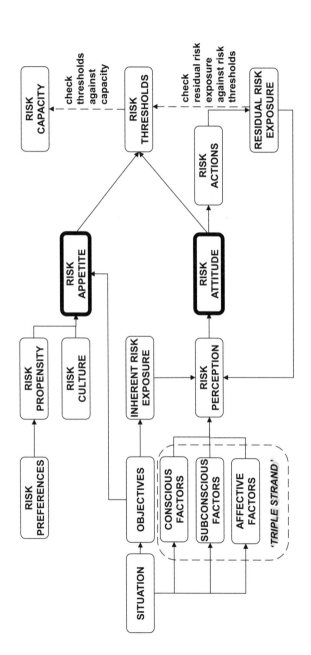

Figure 4.3   The Risk Appetite-Risk Attitude (RARA) Model

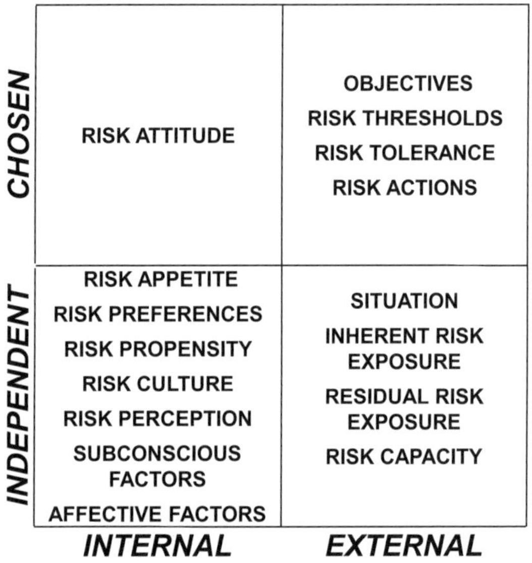

	INTERNAL	EXTERNAL
CHOSEN	RISK ATTITUDE	OBJECTIVES RISK THRESHOLDS RISK TOLERANCE RISK ACTIONS
INDEPENDENT	RISK APPETITE RISK PREFERENCES RISK PROPENSITY RISK CULTURE RISK PERCEPTION SUBCONSCIOUS FACTORS AFFECTIVE FACTORS	SITUATION INHERENT RISK EXPOSURE RESIDUAL RISK EXPOSURE RISK CAPACITY

Figure 4.4   Classifying elements in the RARA Model

The RARA Model allows us to see the interaction between the two central concepts of risk appetite and risk attitude, which act as mediating factors between a wide range of inputs and the key outcomes. We've seen that risk appetite is an internal tendency to take risk in a given situation, and that it is influenced by individual risk propensity and group risk culture, both of which are also internal factors. All of these factors are also hard to influence, so they tend to produce outcomes that are unmanaged, unless there is some intentional or deliberate intervention. This means that when we set risk thresholds as an external expression of risk appetite, there is no guarantee that those thresholds will be appropriate in the circumstances, either when compared to the overall risk capacity, or in support of achieving the required objectives.

Fortunately risk *appetite* is not the only influence on risk thresholds. The RARA Model shows that risk *attitude* also affects the setting of risk thresholds. And the classification of elements in the RARA Model (Figure 4.4) shows something quite striking about risk attitude. Although many of the factors exist internally within individuals and groups, only one can be actively and deliberately chosen: risk attitude. All other internal factors in the RARA Model exist independently, without human intervention or control.

This unique nature of risk attitude gives it a special role in the way the RARA Model works to set appropriate risk thresholds. Since risk attitude is a choice, it provides a control point where we can modify the outcome that naturally arises from our risk appetite. In other words, without any intervention or control, risk appetite will result in us defining a set of risk thresholds that may or may not be suitable. If the resulting thresholds are OK, then we can go ahead and use them as part of our approach to decision-making and risk management. But if the risk thresholds that arise from our risk appetite produce unhelpful or inappropriate behaviour, then we can proactively and intentionally intervene by choosing a different risk attitude that leads to modified risk thresholds.

USING THE RARA MODEL

Throughout this chapter we've built a coherent model using the various risk-related terms that are involved when people are trying to decide how much risk to take in a given situation. We've taken the two central factors of risk appetite and risk attitude, and shown how each of the other factors relate to them. One side-effect produced by this analysis is a clear taxonomy of risk-related terms, which we hope will remove the confusion and inconsistency so often found in this area. The complete taxonomy is presented in Table 4.1. This lists each of the risk-related terms and shows how they fit together.

Table 4.1   Taxonomy of risk-related terms

Definitions of risk-related terms
Risk: Uncertainty that matters
Risk actions: Actions taken to respond to risk exposure, ideally as part of a structured risk process
Risk appetite: Tendency of an individual or group to take risk in a given situation
Risk attitude: Chosen response of an individual or group to a given risky situation, influenced by risk perception
Risk capacity: Ability of an entity to bear risk, quantified against objectives
Risk culture: Shared beliefs, values and knowledge of a group about risk
Risk exposure: A measure of the overall effect of identified risks on objectives. Risk exposure may be expressed quantitatively or qualitatively. **Inherent risk exposure** is the level of risk exposure that exists before risk actions have been implemented. **Residual risk exposure** is the level of risk exposure remaining after agreed risk actions have been implemented
Risk perception: View of risky situation by individual or group, influenced by 'triple strand' (conscious, subconscious and affective) factors
Risk preference: Those aspects of an individual's personality and motivation that influence their risk propensity
Risk propensity: Tendency of an individual to take risk in general, informed by inherent risk preferences
Risk thresholds: Quantified measures that represent upper and lower limits of acceptable uncertainty against each objective

Risk tolerance: The acceptable variance around an objective (an alternative expression of risk thresholds)

Relationships between terms in the risk taxonomy

Individuals are characterised by a general propensity to take **risk** (**risk propensity**), reflecting their inherent risk preferences.

Organisations and groups have a shared **risk culture** reflecting their shared approach to **risk**.

A **situation** arises within which individuals and groups choose one or more **objectives** that they wish to achieve. Individuals and groups develop a perception of the **risk exposure** associated with this situation (**risk perception**), influenced by the **triple strand** of conscious, subconscious and affective factors.

Risk attitude is a chosen response of individuals or groups to a specific **situation** and the associated **objectives**, influenced by **risk perception**. Risk attitude influences the choice of **risk thresholds** and the nature of **risk actions**.

Risk appetite is the inherent tendency of an individual or group to take risk in relation to a specific **situation** and the associated **objectives**, influenced by the **risk propensity** of individual's and/or the organisational **risk culture**.

Risk appetite is expressed via one or more measurable **risk thresholds**, which are quantified in terms of **objectives** (or **risk tolerances**).

Risk thresholds are derived from **risk appetite** and influenced by the chosen **risk attitudes** of stakeholders. They are validated against the overall **risk capacity** of the organisation, to ensure that it is not exceeded. If the total theoretical maximum of all risk thresholds is greater than the overall risk capacity, risk thresholds should be reviewed and modified.

Risk actions are taken in response to the perceived level of **risk exposure** associated with the situation, driven by the chosen **risk attitude**. The results of those actions are evaluated against the defined risk thresholds to ensure that residual risk exposure remains below the threshold and within tolerance limits. If necessary the chosen risk attitude may be modified to support different risk actions, in order to maintain an acceptable risk exposure.

Our main reason for considering these factors however was not to produce a taxonomy or even to construct the RARA Model. It was to answer the key question 'How much risk should we take?' The rest of our book takes the RARA Model and shows how to use it in practice. First we look at how to apply the RARA Model to make risk-informed decisions (Chapter 5), using three incremental scenarios and four worked examples to illustrate the process. In Chapter 6 we explore what can be measured (and what can't) as we try to make good decisions. And finally Chapter 7 provides a step-by-step guide to allow individuals and organisations to apply the ideas behind the RARA Model in order to achieve better risk-informed decision-making.

The RARA Model gives us the context we need to make sense of the various factors that are at work in this area. Now we can turn to the practicalities of what to do and how to do it.

 # Applying the RARA Model: Making Risk-Informed Decisions

Now that we have a clear definition of risk-related terms and a model of how they inter-relate (the RARA Model), we can start the practical task of applying that model to help decision-makers make better risk-informed decisions.

We start by recognising that it's really important for people who are charged with making decisions on behalf of others to do the very best they can to safeguard the collective objectives of stakeholders. All decisions are made in the face of risk – uncertainties that would matter to objectives if they occurred. But it is a gamble to try and make good decisions in risky and important situations by default and there is a way that you can gamble less and secure more appropriate outcomes, more of the time. This can be done by understanding two things:

1. How the concepts of risk appetite and risk attitude work together,

2. How they can be managed through the proxy measure of risk thresholds.

In our deconstruction of risk-related terms in Chapter 4 we have shown how the concepts of risk appetite and risk attitude are different. We demonstrated why they need to be considered together if they are to be useful in shaping organisational outcomes to enable you to take an appropriate amount of risk and put in place appropriate controls. Reconstructing the terms to show how they work together in the RARA Model has provided a framework for considering how much risk would be too much risk to take in situations in your organisation that warrant particular care. It is also a framework for helping you decide on the most appropriate levers to ensure that the decisions you make today deliver the results you want in the future.

In this chapter, we will build some worked examples to show how to apply the RARA Model in practice. We have chosen four examples of risky decisions to provide sufficient context to apply our thinking to different types of decision-making challenges.

Let's start by illustrating how a consideration of risk appetite and risk attitude improves the appropriateness of risk thresholds. The best way to do this is by considering how the RARA Model might work in the absence of considering risk appetite and risk attitude. Here are three different scenarios:

1. An *Unmanaged* scenario, in which risk thresholds are set by the organisation with no conscious or intentional reference to risk appetite or risk attitude.

2. A *Constrained* scenario, in which risk thresholds are consciously modified by an understanding of the inherent risk appetite and checked against the risk capacity.

3. An *Informed* scenario, which involves setting risk thresholds only after choosing a risk attitude that takes into account

how the perceptions of key stakeholders are altered by the triple strand of influences.

These three scenarios can be seen as representing increasing maturity in the application of risk-informed decision-making. They demonstrate how the process works in principle. We'll describe the scenarios first, and our four worked examples will then follow.

THE UNMANAGED SCENARIO

Figure 5.1 shows part of the RARA Model. It illustrates what is being considered when risk thresholds are set without considering risk appetite or risk attitude in the decision-making process. We call this the Unmanaged Scenario, and at first sight there appears to be nothing wrong with the sequence of events. It describes a set of actions that most decision-making groups would recognise as familiar. However, there is a problem with following this scenario to set risk thresholds.

Although risk thresholds in this scenario are the proxy for 'how much risk is too much risk' (as in all other scenarios) – because the only influence on the thresholds are the objectives in the situation, the thresholds set here may be culturally inappropriate, and not understood and shared by the stakeholders involved with the decision. This may lead to those stakeholders taking inappropriate (possibly wasteful) risk actions.

In the Unmanaged Scenario, risk thresholds are influenced primarily by the objectives in the situation. This can be done by using standard 'one size fits all' practices of agreeing a tolerance around a target, such as ±10 per cent variation around a budgetary provision, or ±1 per cent variation around a customer satisfaction

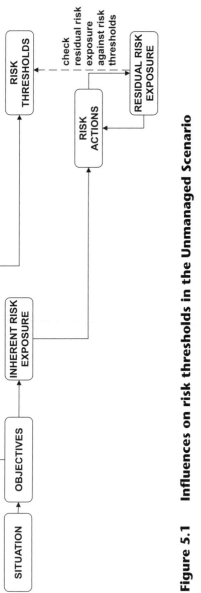

Figure 5.1   Influences on risk thresholds in the Unmanaged Scenario

level. Alternatively, unmanaged risk thresholds can be set simply by taking a 'gut-feel' guess at what sounds reasonable.

Although risks exist, and may be noticed to a greater or lesser degree by stakeholders, stakeholder perceptions of exposure to risk are not considered when setting risk thresholds in the Unmanaged Scenario. This results in risk actions being taken (or not taken) by stakeholders, based on their unexplored perception, and resulting in a residual risk exposure that someone could and should monitor vs. the risk thresholds (and hopefully someone will actually do that). Where residual risk exposure *is* monitored against risk thresholds, the only control available is to try to keep residual exposure within a threshold that has been arbitrarily set in the first place. Unfortunately we've come across some situations where no monitoring against risk thresholds takes place.

This scenario is called Unmanaged, because the way risk thresholds are set is not actively managed, and the risk actions leading to the residual exposure are also unmanaged in the context of the overall decision. It is of course possible that the unmanaged approach may result in suitable risk thresholds being set, but this is likely to be the result of good luck rather than good judgement.

So how might you improve on this approach? One important step would be to deliberately consider risk appetite and the factors that influence it – we call this the Constrained Scenario.

THE CONSTRAINED SCENARIO

Figure 5.2 shows that the Constrained Scenario uses more of the overall RARA Model than the Unmanaged Scenario.

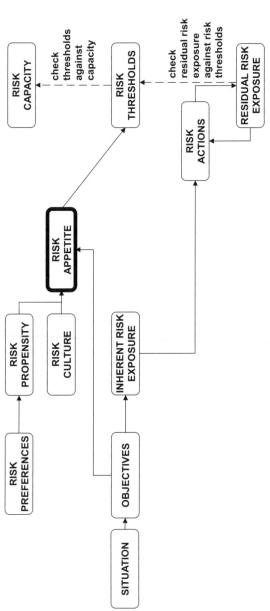

Figure 5.2   Influences on risk thresholds in the Constrained Scenario

It illustrates the influences when risk thresholds are set after explicitly considering the tendency of the organisation or individual to take risk in a particular situation – that is, risk appetite. It also shows the overt step of checking risk thresholds against the organisation's risk capacity to make sure that the amount of uncertainty represented by the risk threshold can be borne and this usually means paying a price to bear the risk. These are positive actions to take. The Constrained Scenario, however, omits the parts of the RARA Model that deal with risk attitude. There is still no logical point of control in the decision-making process. The risk thresholds chosen here are likely to be more appropriate and understood than those that would result from the Unmanaged Scenario, but a logic for the choice of risk actions is still missing, so inappropriate and possibly wasteful risk actions may still be adopted.

In the Constrained Scenario, risk thresholds are not only influenced by the objectives of the situation. They are also influenced by the tendency of the key decision-makers to take risk (the risk propensity of key individuals shaped by their inherent risk preferences) and by the shared beliefs and values of the group when taking decisions in such situations (the risk culture). Of course the risk propensity of key individuals and the risk culture of the organisation might be implicitly built into the unmanaged practices of setting standard plus-or-minus tolerances around target objectives. However, in the Constrained Scenario, these influences are explicitly taken into account when setting the risk threshold. For example, it may be our usual practice to set a ±10 per cent variation around a budgetary provision, but perhaps in this particular situation we might be uncomfortable with this, believing that it does not reflect the current organisational context for the decision. Instead we may judge it more appropriate to keep residual risk exposure within a threshold of ±20 per cent variation, or perhaps we might prefer ±5 per cent variation. Using the analogy with physical appetite introduced in Chapter 4 again here, we are deciding whether our hunger is for a decision that would represent a large (600-gram/20-ounce) T-bone steak or a small (150 gram/4 ounce) petit-filet rather than our usual 400-gram/12-ounce sirloin. Whether in the case of physical appetite or risk appetite, we need a quantified measure that is externally visible to stand as a proxy for our internal risk appetite.

The explicit step of checking whether the organisation is able to handle the degree of variation around the target represented by the risk thresholds makes sure that decisions are not disconnected from wider portfolio, organisational decisions. It would be irresponsible for individual decisions based on judgements that expose the organisation to risk to be made without consideration of the collection of other decisions that also introduce risk to organisational objectives. Whether our decision represents a hunger for the small, medium or large piece of meat, the organisation only has the equivalent of one animal to draw from. The aggregate variation represented by risk thresholds in a portfolio of work must fit within the overall risk capacity of the organisation.

Whilst this judgement on the setting of risk thresholds is at least an improvement on taking a standard or 'gut-feel' approach as in the Unmanaged Scenario, it still does not take any account of stakeholder perceptions of the inherent risk exposure in the situation.

This scenario is called Constrained, because the way risk thresholds are set is constrained by the tendency of the key decision-makers in a given organisational culture to take risk in a particular situation, even though this tendency is largely invisible. Judgements are also constrained by the organisation's ability to bear the risk associated with the extremes of the thresholds. This approach may still result in inappropriate thresholds, for example, ones that are too conservative and end up restricting growth because of historical risk thresholds to pursue previous, less risky, growth strategies; or ones that are too liberal that reflect the desire of the organisation for profitable growth, but allow a level of variation that does not make overall business sense. The risk actions taken, based on stakeholder perceptions of risks and leading to the residual exposure, remain unmanaged in the context of the overall decision.

The Informed Scenario takes the last step to building a risk-informed, decision-making system by adding chosen risk attitude back into the picture, explicitly considering the influence of stakeholders and their perception of risks, and so creating the ability to exert active and intentional control.

THE INFORMED SCENARIO

It is important to take proper account of risk appetite and risk capacity when setting risk thresholds, which the Constrained Scenario does, but this is not the whole story. In every case, it is *people* who take decisions on what level of risk exposure is appropriate, working either as individuals or in groups. Despite some views to the contrary, people are not dispassionate rational actors who make decisions based on perfect economic utility. Instead we bring a range of overt and covert influences to our decision-making, including subconscious cognitive biases and psychological heuristics, as well as affective emotional factors. It is not possible to set appropriate risk thresholds without considering these influences on our perception of risk, which in turn affects individual and group risk attitude. We therefore need to add risk attitude back into the picture, producing the Informed Scenario that brings us back to the full RARA Model (see Figure 5.3 that repeats Figure 4.3 in Chapter 4).

The big difference between the Constrained and Informed level of maturity in risk-informed decision-making is the role of risk attitude and its influence on two things:

1. Deliberate and informed setting of risk thresholds, and

2. Control of risk actions to keep residual risk exposure within risk thresholds, as a mediator between risk perception and those risk actions.

Risk thresholds in the Informed Scenario are set only after considering the risk attitude that the decision-makers choose to adopt (based on the perception of the inherent risks). Let's say that in the Constrained Scenario, the organisation set a risk threshold of ±20 per cent around a budgetary target for an investment, on the basis of:

- The situation and objectives (growth in a new market)

- The appetite for risk that fitted with key decision-makers' preferences and the organisation's norms

- The organisational capacity to bear that variance around the target.

In the Informed Scenario this target would be challenged, and then either validated or changed by considering explicitly the stakeholder's perception of the inherent risks.

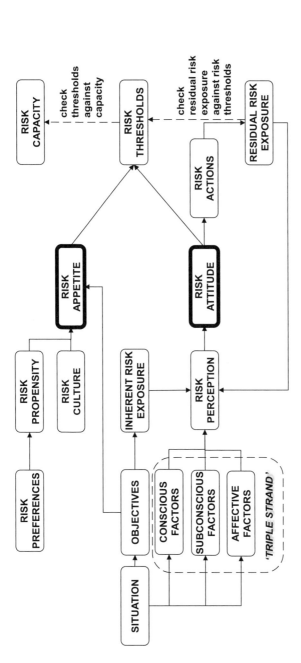

Figure 5.3   Influences on risk thresholds in the Informed Scenario

So following the example through, although the risk thresholds set are at ±20 per cent around the budgetary target for an investment, it might be that the risks identified have the potential for an outcome outside those thresholds, say a 30–40 per cent increase on the budgetary target but with little upside (say 5–10 per cent less spend).

The simple response, in the Constrained Scenario, would be to say that risk actions should be taken to reduce residual exposure so that the possible variation in cost remains within the ± 20 per cent target.

In the Informed Scenario, there is another perspective, and that is to factor risk attitude into the way that risk thresholds are set.

The most appropriate, risk-informed judgement would be for decision-makers to choose the upper risk threshold based on the cost that would return the lowest acceptable return for the company. For example, if the business case would still be positive with a +50 per cent upper risk threshold, then this threshold could be set, and decision-makers would then adopt a risk-tolerant attitude to a risk register that could increase costs by +30–40 per cent. If, on the other hand, the business case was marginal at +20 per cent, then a more risk-averse attitude would be needed to drive actions to reduce exposure.

There is no 'right' answer in such situations – only an appropriate answer in a particular situation. The RARA Model is designed to help decision-makers to understand all the influences that matter so they can consciously and deliberately set risk thresholds at an appropriate level.

The Informed Scenario includes the influence of risk attitude alongside risk appetite, showing how managed risk attitude offers a point of choice and intervention in the decision-making process. The link between residual risk exposure and risk perception allows the chosen risk attitude to be changed in order to keep actions in line with risk thresholds. As a result we can best align risk thresholds with objectives, make sure the plan is coherent with the prevailing risk culture, and provide appropriate targeting and effectiveness of risk actions.

FOUR WORKED EXAMPLES

Now let's see how this progressive approach to setting appropriate risk thresholds might work in our four examples of risky decisions.

We'll refer to our example risky decisions as *My Decision*, the *Operational Decision*, the *Strategic Decision* and the *Community Decision*. You'll see not only how the Unmanaged, Constrained and Informed scenarios might play out in each decision, but how the RARA Model can be applied at multiple, connected levels across organisations. The concept of multiple levels of risk appetite within any organisation also has important implications when it comes to putting this into practice, as we'll explore in Chapter 7.

My Decision. Suppose that I have to decide whether to invest more of my income in a financial investment product of some type, with the objective of saving for the future and providing a 'reasonable' return on my investment. What would be 'reasonable'? How much risk would be too much risk for me to take?

Operational Decision. Imagine you are the manager of a major manufacturing site within a multinational company. As part of the annual planning round you need to make plans for how you'll manage delivery of corporate objectives. We'll just consider three of them here – operational safety, productivity and employee satisfaction. Do risk thresholds apply here? How can you explicitly consider risk as part of your decision-making process?

Strategic Decision. Here we focus on a large investment in the public sector – a major new rail project to upgrade the line between the two biggest cities in the country. What part do risk thresholds play during the up-front investment decision-making process? And what part during delivery of the project once it has been approved?

Community Decision. How shall we work as a community in Our Town of 10,000 people to build a sense of pride for the environment and opportunities for inhabitants to contribute and to care for each other? How can informed risk thresholds help us do the right things?

So far in this chapter we've described three incremental scenarios that illustrate how risk appetite and risk attitude should work when we are trying to set appropriate risk thresholds. We can now apply those three scenarios to our four example decisions to show the effect of risk appetite and risk attitude in practice. As we've done earlier, let's look at the three steps in turn, from the Unmanaged Scenario through the Constrained Scenario and on to the Informed Scenario.

UNMANAGED SCENARIO

We start by looking at how each of the four example decisions might be made in the absence of any active consideration of either risk appetite or risk attitude.

1. In **My Decision**, if I was making my investment decision using the type of gut-feel approach that the Unmanaged Scenario involves, it's unlikely that I would consider risk thresholds explicitly. In this example, there are two relevant risk thresholds. One relates to the amount of money I'm prepared to invest each month without putting my other commitments at risk, while still maximising my opportunity to get the best return from my expendable income. The other risk threshold can be seen as the forecast uncertainty with the outcomes of the investment that I make, whether in a pension fund, a portfolio of stocks, or other financial product.

   The primary influence is likely to be what my financial advisor is proposing that I do, based on their analysis of my personal circumstances, my ability to invest, and my need to make provision for funds in the future. Only I can decide what I can afford to invest, and the timing of this (I may have a monthly fixed income and my ability to invest is known, or I may have variable income and may want to be able to vary investments). Regarding the risks in the financial product chosen, I may be passive and not actively engage in analysis of the risks involved. Once the investment is made, what risk actions might I take? Am I proactive in deciding whether to keep investing at the current rate if the forecast outcomes of the investment change, or if my ability to pay changes? Or do I not pay attention to these things and just keep paying the direct debit through my bank regardless?

2. It's possible that risk thresholds may not be explicitly considered in the **Operational Decision** either, although in large organisations this is probably not the case.

    Large organisations are most likely to have targets for objectives such as operational safety, productivity and employee satisfaction, but do they have thresholds that are thought through? Maybe no thresholds are set at all – there's just a target and as a manager your bonus depends on you meeting or improving on it. Or maybe there are thresholds, but they are just an arbitrary plus and/or minus tolerance around the target. If this is the case, how then do you decide how much of your managerial effort to put into identifying and managing risks that might cause performance out of tolerance? Thresholds set in this way may be inappropriate. Should you to tolerate the same variance around the target for employee satisfaction as you would for operational safety? Probably not. Thresholds may also conflict and drive inappropriate behaviour; for example, in a manufacturing facility, the operational safety in most organisations would be a higher priority than productivity or employee satisfaction. Managerial actions to improve productivity may encourage unsafe working. Actions to insist on safe working may be interpreted by staff as annoying and pernickety, rather than in their interests, thus reducing employee satisfaction. It is important to understand the amount of risk that can be tolerated for all objectives, and the Unmanaged Scenario does not provide this.

3. It is particularly important in a project scenario to understand the relative priority of objectives, so you can

focus management attention on the critical matters. In the **Strategic Decision**, how certain do decision-makers need to be about estimates of cost and schedule before they invest public money in a major transportation scheme? In the Unmanaged Scenario, risk thresholds are potentially not considered at all. Work to build a business case for the investment will have taken into account best estimates of cost and the phasing of expenditure (cash out) and benefit streams (value in). In a large public sector scheme such as the Strategic Decision, sophisticated risk modelling may also have taken place, but would risk thresholds be set and used to avoid the scheme being approved with 'too much' risk to objectives included?

4. Finally, the **Community Decision** is the example where it is least likely that risk is considered at all in the Unmanaged Scenario. While objectives in the other three examples were relatively tangible and measurable, objectives seem less tangible in this case, and the very concept of risk thresholds may seem impossible to rationalise. Let's take the objective of building an increased sense of pride in the environment within Our Town. We can certainly describe this objective, and we know it is something we want more of not less of. But how will we judge when we have more civic pride, and when will we know when to act if we have too little? Unfortunately, valid, well-meaning, heroic attempts at improvement in examples like the Community Decision often end up in frustration and arbitrary claims of success or failure because in the Unmanaged Scenario, there is no mechanism for establishing and governing appropriate management.

We can see from these four examples that a lack of understanding of and focus on acceptable levels of risk may lead to inappropriate outcomes. Next we'll see how the Constrained Scenario improves the situation when risk appetite is considered explicitly.

CONSTRAINED SCENARIO

Rather than risk thresholds (if considered at all) being established based on understanding objectives, the Constrained Scenario builds in two checks (see Figure 5.2). Firstly we build in the effect of risk appetite, the invisible manifestation of our hunger for risk. Secondly the risk capacity of the organisation is considered to make sure that our hunger for risk doesn't exceed our ability to bear it. Let's look first at the effect of risk appetite then go on to see how the concept of risk capacity applies.

Risk appetite is shaped by inherent tendencies to take risk and these tendencies exist at multiple levels. Individual risk preferences shape an individual's propensity to take risk. Organisational risk preferences are embedded in the organisation's culture for risk – 'the way we do things around here'. If we understand this we'll see that in every decision in every situation, risk appetite and therefore risk thresholds are influenced across the board. This means that there will always be influences from the key decision-makers, but these will be felt in the context of the 'organisation' – even if that organisation is a family or a community and not a 'formal' line or project structure. Knowledge of organisational culture tells us that some organisations have strong, cohesive cultures, cemented by common practices, rituals and symbols that sustain purpose and meaning. In such strongly binding organisational cultures, the risk culture is likely to be understood and institutionalised. Other organisations spend less time building cohesive values and ways of working, believing that value is created through differences, and knowing that less tightly coupled systems are more flexible and more easily adapted when needed. Risk culture in weaker organisational cultures may not even be recognised, with the dominant influence on risk appetite being the preferences of the individuals involved.

How can we explicitly consider risk appetite in our four example decisions, in the way that the Constrained Scenario describes?

1. In **My Decision**, my risk preferences, and therefore my propensity for risk are quite different from my husband's. Where I am very likely to take significant risk with an investment, he is naturally more cautious. Because we have very different risk perspectives, the risk culture of our family is not well defined or understood – it does not overtly shape behaviour. This may not be the case if there were strong values and trends in how our wider families have behaved in the past, or if there were strong societal norms about the decision (for example, if the decision was about investing in car insurance). Interestingly also, the risk propensity of my financial adviser (or the one he adopts when selling) is also relevant in the decision-making process – shaping my judgement of how much risk I am taking by choosing a certain option. This is the case even though he is not part of our family risk culture. All external consultants or advisers who are involved in decision-making bring their tendencies to take risk to the decision-making table, but they may be presenting a view that is counter to the prevailing risk culture.

2. The **Operational Decision** is focused on setting risk thresholds for operational safety, productivity and employee satisfaction for a manufacturing site within a multinational firm's annual business planning process. It is most likely that organisational norms and the risk culture will be the dominant influence on risk appetite and therefore risk thresholds. Of course, the manager who needs to make and sell plans to more senior management will have his or her own views on how much risk is too much to objectives, as will the rest of the management team on site and the people who work for them. These individual views would have more of an effect if the organisational norms were less strong. We know actual examples of companies where the willingness to take risk with operational safety is very small and where this objective would definitely be prioritised ahead of productivity. A culture that is focused on 'zero harm' will spend time and money on reducing health and safety risk that others would not do. Such firms often argue that this approach also results in high productivity and higher employee satisfaction. Perhaps they may be right?

3. The Constrained Scenario in the **Strategic Decision** example raises some other points. The relative influences of individual decision-makers and the organisation's risk culture remain, but in a strategic investment decision, the logic of relying on organisational norms could have less use. The decision to invest public money in an expensive, long-term scheme where certainty about costs and timescales is low is different from a decision (in the same organisation) to upgrade track and points on an existing line. The risk thresholds set for the latter would need to be much tighter than the former. Risk appetite alone may constrain decision-making in an inappropriate way.

4. Does Our Town have a risk culture that would influence the **Community Decision**? Probably not. As in **My Decision**, the influence of individual stakeholders is likely to be greater than any collective sense of how much risk is enough or too much. This time, though, there are many individual stakeholders, probably with conflicting views. The prevailing risk appetite here would be a feature of the dominant stakeholders, maybe the elected leaders in a democracy, or people who have lots of respect as community players and influence with others through their history and embedded relationships.

Just as Our Town is unlikely to have an understood risk culture, it is also unlikely to have any agreed risk capacity, that is, ability to bear certain levels of 'lack of pride' or 'failure to care for others'. In such circumstances, risk thresholds are most difficult to get right. By contrast, in formal organisations such as in the Strategic and Operational decisions, risk capacity will be calculable, based on balance sheets or Treasury funding. In My Decision, risk capacity is probably the best understood because the 'organisation' (my family) is smaller and (you would hope) more intimate with how much risk could be borne if everything went wrong.

So, although the Constrained Scenario is better than the Unmanaged, none of these decisions can set risk thresholds with confidence without considering, not just risk appetite, but also risk attitude. We have argued in the RARA Model that risk attitude is the only meaningful control point that decision-makers have. This is illustrated next.

INFORMED SCENARIO

There is a general principle that applies here to all of our examples. Choosing appropriate risk thresholds requires the stakeholders to talk about risk, about the influences on perception of risk for the various options open, and about the most appropriate way forward in the situation. Decisions are not informed if they are made in isolation of the many and varied sources of information, funds and support from the people involved. In the Informed Scenario, the risk thresholds that are chosen can never be validated as 'correct', but they can be verified as fitting within the risk capacity and representing an appropriate way forward for the stakeholders involved in that organisational context. Ongoing checking of risk exposure against thresholds will then lead to appropriate action to maintain residual levels of risk at an appropriate level – neither too much, nor too little (given that reducing risk and/or increasing certainty costs money).

So is it important to talk about perceptions of risk, and about perceptions of how much risk would be too much risk to take. We know from our work, and that of others, that risk attitudes adopted are personal (we don't all think the same way) and situational (I adopt different attitudes at different times). We know that nothing is 'real' when thinking about potential future events. All we can do is to understand what might be driving our thoughts, feelings and behaviour.

So finally let's see how the Informed Scenario plays out in our four example decisions.

1. In **My Decision**, how much risk do I see in different financial products I might buy? Is my perception different from my partner's, or my financial advisers? Maybe I've

had a bad experience with investments in the past and my trust in the potential value of a new investment is tarnished. Maybe my partner has a different perception of the risks involved in the decision due to a fear of not having enough expendable income now, believing that the future will take care of itself? There are innumerable permutations of influences. We can only make the right decisions for us, at that time, by talking through perspectives and making an informed choice.

2. In a small organisation, like a family, talking things through is relatively easy to achieve. In a large organisation things are more difficult. Not everyone can be consulted. Here we have to rely on understanding who the key stakeholders (or representatives of key constituencies) are and liaise with them.

In the **Operational Decision**, the management team needs to decide on annual targets, budgets and suitable risk thresholds for operational safety, productivity and employee satisfaction. Let's assume that the organisation has methods already in place for measuring results for all the objectives, and that actual results for past years exist. To adopt an Informed position, the manager would not simply take each individual objective and adopt the company targets and thresholds as standard. An Informed approach would be to bring together representatives of key stakeholders, including the management team, employee reps and maybe representatives from relevant corporate functions such as health and safety, human resources and/or technical services. This group can look at past performance and the 'standard' targets, discuss the specific context in the plant and the associated risks to achieving those targets, consider the relationships between objectives and decide appropriate thresholds for that situation at that time.

It is quite possible that narrow risk thresholds and a risk-averse attitude to ensuring human health and safety might be adopted, but wider thresholds and a risk-seeking attitude that is relatively more comfortable with uncertainty could be adopted for productivity. A risk-neutral attitude may be agreed for employee satisfaction where managers are happy to take a chance in the short-term in order to secure longer-term results. This approach would make the targets personal and situational, not arbitrary. It would also allow differences in viewpoint to be explored, leaving a richer and more informed perspective on which risks need to be managed to enable the best performance for all stakeholders. Perhaps this is an approach with which you are already familiar? Our observations are that managers will recognise that they have internally gone through the process of deciding 'how much risk is enough' for their objectives, but have not validated their viewpoints with those of their colleagues and staff in any systematic way. This is a recipe for confusion, frustration and potential disappointment as different people strive for different levels of control and different outcomes. It doesn't have to be that way.

3. The number and diversity of stakeholders in the **Strategic Decision** will be yet wider. Engaging with stakeholders to explore perceptions and perspectives will require more formal approaches, probably involving workshops, focus groups, and other methods of gaining rich information from different constituencies. The decision to be supported is not just whether to go ahead with the new rail link, but the appropriate timescale for development, the

appropriate amount of money to spend, the appropriate safety, environmental, regulatory and quality standards to commit to, and the appropriate level of societal benefit that would need to be realised. Risk thresholds are necessary for all these objectives. They will be set of course (even if only in the mind of a few people), but will they be appropriate? Although engaging with stakeholders in such a situation is time-consuming and 'messy' (the only thing certain is that there will be no consensus of opinion!), decision-makers have little option but to do so if they are to invest public funds wisely.

It would be normal for wide consultation to take place in an example such as the **Strategic Decision**. However, such processes rarely appear to support decision-making by explicitly setting risk thresholds or deciding on risk actions based on an understanding of risk appetite and risk attitude. The RARA Model provides a way of channelling stakeholder discussions, providing an understanding of the key concepts and why they matter. It also provides a framework within which stakeholders can challenge other perceptions (for example, of the inherent risk in the situation) and see the impact of changes in one part of the model on risk thresholds. It is vital to challenge perceptions in order to ensure that judgements about current exposure and thresholds are not systematically biased by the risk attitude of key stakeholders, and we have written about this extensively elsewhere (Hillson and Murray-Webster, 2007; Murray-Webster and Hillson, 2008). What we add here is the recognition that it's important within organisations to have a mechanism to channel discussions about subjective topics such as the existence and potential future impact of risks if decision-makers are to make wise judgements. The RARA Model provides that mechanism.

We should note here that engaging diverse stakeholders to share perspectives and come to collective decisions is skilled work that is enabled by expert facilitation. Good risk facilitators make it easier for decision-makers to navigate the risk analysis and management process and avoid the pitfalls that are presented by the psychological biases that combine to influence risk attitudes. As evidenced by the body of literature on behavioural economics, it is all too easy for biases such as groupthink, the anchoring bias or the illusion of knowledge to skew the process so that managers pay too much attention to irrational factors. There is also the danger of cultural organisational factors such as the hierarchy, or the formality of governance to get in the way of the decision, especially if the most senior person has a strongly-held view. There are many influences on risk attitude, but the outcomes exist on a spectrum that ranges from highly cautious behaviour and discomfort with risk through to high comfort with risk and risk-seeking behaviour (see Figure 3.1). The risk facilitator can help in the selection of the appropriate attitude for a given situation and thus enable suitable risk thresholds to be agreed.

So because risk attitude can be chosen, risk thresholds can be modified in an intentional way to support appropriate risk-taking. This helps us ensure that whilst we don't take on too much risk, we have the best chance of achieving our objectives.

4. In the final example, that of the **Community Decision**, we no longer focus on the task of *setting* risk thresholds in the Informed Scenario. Instead, our aim is to ensure there is an *ongoing fit* between risk exposure and risk thresholds. This involves adopting a risk attitude that

focuses on achieving the right amount of certainty in a given situation.

Let's assume that a representative selection of stakeholders has decided on targets, a measurement system and risk thresholds for the objective of people 'caring for others' within Our Town. Based on the current situation in the town and the risks that would influence progress, a number of actions have been taken. Some involve communication, such as promoting a positive message through posters, education in schools and advertising stories of good practice. Others are controls that focus on exposing antisocial behaviour and helping to make it culturally unacceptable in the town. These actions need to be repeated to be effective. In an Informed Scenario, stakeholders would use the RARA Model to help them focus on their points of control – the choice of risk attitude and the choice of risk actions to bring performance and residual exposure in line with chosen risk thresholds. If things were going well, the town leadership team might decide that targets could be extended, and thresholds reduced without further controlling actions. If things aren't going well, a more risk-averse attitude (discomfort with risks that would detract from the 'caring for others' objective) would need to be adopted, with different actions to sell the benefits of caring to the community.

SUMMARY

This chapter has used scenarios and examples to bring the ideas behind the RARA Model to life. The three scenarios of Unmanaged, Constrained and Informed have been explained, showing how the concepts of risk appetite and risk attitude help in setting risk thresholds that represent a tolerable level of risk to the organisation, and also how they help us to manage our risk exposure to stay within those thresholds.

Our four examples of My Decision, the Operational Decision, the Strategic Decision and the Community Decision have been used to illustrate different aspects of putting the RARA Model into practice. In particular we have highlighted the multilayered nature of both risk appetite and risk attitude, given their application at individual person, small team, wider organisational and societal levels. We have also highlighted the imperative to engage diverse stakeholders and find a way of channelling and challenging perspectives with the aim of finding suitable paths through complex decisions.

The RARA Model provides a logical framework that skilled facilitators can use to bring together stakeholders to focus on planning and decision-making in risky and important situations, so the group can be confident that they have a shared understanding of how much risk to take. In smaller, more local groups, including families making big decisions, the model will help the people involved to make sense of the uncertainty and risk dimension of their decisions and move forward in an Informed way. No model can bring certainty, but application of the RARA Model can prevent uncertainty wreaking havoc in your situation.

In this chapter we have applied the RARA Model to four worked examples, showing how can we can have an informed decision-making process for setting risk thresholds by starting from an unmanaged decision, adding first the effects of risk appetite and risk capacity, and then adding risk attitude. We will continue with the practicalities of working with the RARA Model in Chapter 6 by exploring what can be measured (and what can't) as we try to make good decisions. Specifically in that chapter we will continue to clarify the language used in this tricky area of management. This will then lead into Chapter 7 and our step-by-step guide that enables individuals and organisations to apply the ideas behind the RARA Model in order to achieve better risk-informed decision-making.

REFERENCES

Hillson D. A. and Murray-Webster R. 2007. *Understanding and Managing Risk Attitude* (second edition). Aldershot, UK: Gower.

Murray-Webster R. and Hillson D. A. 2008. *Managing Group Risk Attitude*. Aldershot, UK: Gower.

⑥ Practical Implications: What Can We Measure?

In our description and application of the RARA Model so far, we have focused on risk thresholds as the directly measurable articulation of risk appetite and risk attitude, that is, 'how much risk will we take in this situation?' In Chapter 5 we used practical examples to show that if risk thresholds are to be useful in guiding decision-making, then they need to be informed by an understanding of the influences on risk appetite (the things that affect the tendency of the group or individual to take risk) and the influences on risk attitude (factors affecting perception of risk). We used four worked examples across the three scenarios – Unmanaged, Constrained and Informed – to illustrate how each element of the RARA Model works as part of a coherent whole.

But are risk thresholds (or the synonymous term risk tolerances) the only things we can measure? This is an important question to answer, as organisations that want to improve their risk management need to know what management information and controls they can establish. This chapter explores this topic.

WHAT CAN BE MEASURED AND WHAT MAY ONLY BE UNDERSTOOD?

As noted in Chapter 4, one interesting feature of the RARA Model is that some factors are internal, existing only within individuals and/or groups of people, while others exist externally of the people involved in the situation. We can also divide the various risk-related factors that make up the complete RARA Model into those that are capable of being controlled and those which are an inherent feature of the situation and therefore exist independently of human control. Figure 4.4 classified the elements of the RARA Model using these two dimensions of existing within (internal) or outside (external) the people involved; and capable of human control (chosen) or inherent to the situation and not controllable (independent). This figure is repeated here as Figure 6.1.

As previously noted, this classification helps us to understand which elements we can observe and potentially measure because they exist outside people as part of the risky situation, and which elements we can only seek to understand because they exist only as perceptions, tendencies or habits within the people involved with the risky and important decision. The classification also points us to those elements that provide a point of control for decision-makers, that is, those elements where a choice can be made as opposed to those elements where decision-makers have no opportunity to directly influence.

Once again, in this chapter, we point out where loose terminology has confused matters in the past, but this time we explain where commonly-used diagnostics or measurement techniques fit into the RARA Model, and how these can help

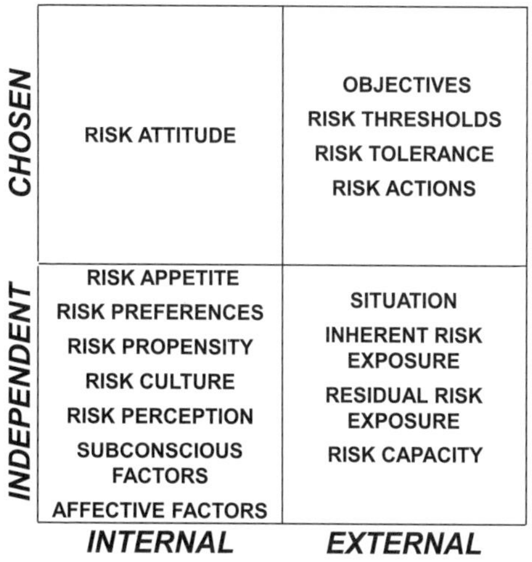

	INTERNAL	EXTERNAL
CHOSEN	RISK ATTITUDE	OBJECTIVES RISK THRESHOLDS RISK TOLERANCE RISK ACTIONS
INDEPENDENT	RISK APPETITE RISK PREFERENCES RISK PROPENSITY RISK CULTURE RISK PERCEPTION SUBCONSCIOUS FACTORS AFFECTIVE FACTORS	SITUATION INHERENT RISK EXPOSURE RESIDUAL RISK EXPOSURE RISK CAPACITY

Figure 6.1   Classification of elements of the RARA Model

you to develop a practical system of making risk-informed decisions in your organisation.

THE UNMANAGED SCENARIO: ONLY TANGIBLE FACTORS

All the variables in the Unmanaged Scenario (shown here as Figure 6.2) are external factors, existing outside individual people or a collective group. Some of these are pre-existing un-chosen factors, for example the situation itself and the inherent risk exposure associated with the situation. Others are chosen by people, for example the objectives in the situation, the risk thresholds and tolerances selected, and risk actions. All the factors in the Unmanaged Scenario can be explicitly observed or articulated. Risk actions can be observed and objectives, risk thresholds and risk tolerances can be expressed in tangible terms.

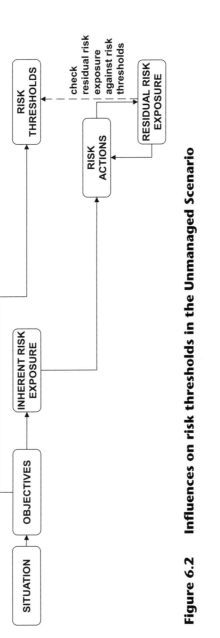

Figure 6.2   Influences on risk thresholds in the Unmanaged Scenario

Because all the factors in the Unmanaged Scenario are visible and measurable, it appears deceptively simple to set risk thresholds using this approach. However, the failure to take proper account of the other factors in the RARA Model, particularly the central mediating factors of risk appetite and risk attitude, means that the resulting risk thresholds are likely to be flawed. If the 'right result' is achieved, then it probably arose more by good luck than good judgement.

THE CONSTRAINED SCENARIO: FACTORS WITH PROXY MEASURES

The Unmanaged Scenario is developed into the Constrained Scenario by the addition of risk appetite and its precedents (risk preferences, risk propensity, risk culture) and by explicitly considering the risk thresholds in the context of the organisation's risk capacity as shown in Figure 6.3. These factors put the Unmanaged Scenario into its proper context, allowing a link to be made between the risk thresholds and factors that exist independently of the specific situation.

The situation, inherent risk exposure and residual risk exposure in the Unmanaged Scenario are pre-existing, un-chosen and can be expressed in tangible terms. This is also the case for risk capacity, introduced in the Constrained Scenario. However, the other factors introduced in the Constrained Scenario are not of this nature.

Risk preferences, risk propensity and risk culture are all internal factors, existing within people or within the collective but intangible ethos of a group of people. They are

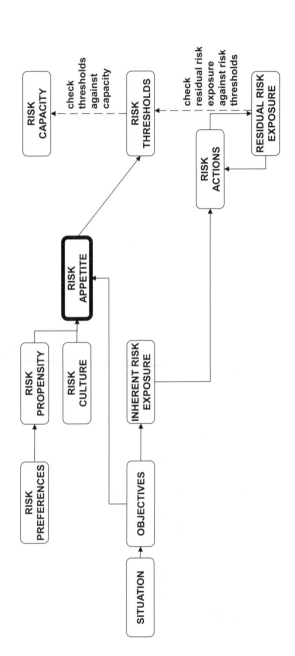

Figure 6.3   Influences on risk thresholds in the Constrained Scenario

not explicitly chosen in each decision-making situation, they exist independently of that decision as deeply-held enduring values and motivations.

There is a significant body of existing work on risk preferences, risk propensity and risk culture that suggests how these factors might be assessed and/or measured. This is too big to review in detail here, but we can summarise the main conclusions. You will see from the information presented that there can be no direct and objective measure of these factors given their existence within people; however, there are some proxy measures that are of some use.

Measuring individual risk preferences and risk propensity. The risk preferences of individuals (as innate motivations) can be determined through the use of psychological instruments that measure personality-related preferences and traits. Such instruments allow an individual to diagnose and reflect upon their likely starting point when faced with a risky and important situation. Table 6.1 summarises a sample of popular diagnostic tools that include some 'measure' of risk-related personality preferences, based on self-assessment questionnaires. All these instruments provide some insights into the risk preferences of individuals that in turn suggest their propensity or tendency to take risks.

In all cases, it would be wrong to say that these instruments could 'measure' risk preferences – although some would make that claim. It would also be wrong to say that such instruments could predict the influence of these preferences on risk appetite or risk attitude given that both of these constructs are highly situational. However, personality preferences are useful for individuals to understand their innate motivations, if only

Table 6.1   Risk-related personality preferences

Diagnostic tool	Risk preferences
Spony Profiling Model™ (Spony, 2003)	• Motivation to seek out risk or to act cautiously when achieving tasks (included as part of a wider assessment).
Myers-Briggs Type Indicator™ (Briggs-Myers and Myers, 1980)	• Motivation to 'keep options open' when decision-making and to prefer to live with uncertainty for a time until a decision needs to be made (part of the Perceiving preference). • Motivation to act quickly to close down options and put in place decisive plans (part of the Judging preference).
Risk-Type Compass™ (Trickey and Stewart, 2010)	• Spontaneous: Uninhibited, excitable, unpredictable and distraught when things go wrong. • Intense: Passionate, apprehensive, defeated by set-backs and self-criticism. • Wary: Anxious, highly organising, need for control and certainty. • Prudent: Cautious, controlled and most comfortable with continuity and familiarity. • Deliberate: Imperturbable and self-confident but never walks into anything unprepared. • Composed: Cool headed, optimistic and seemingly almost oblivious to risk. • Adventurous: Combine a deeply constitutional calmness, impulsivity and willingness to challenge. • Carefree: Unconventional, daring and excitement seeking, their impatience and imprudence.

Table 6.1   Risk-related   personality   preferences
concluded

Diagnostic tool	Risk preferences
Cattell's 16 Personality Factor Model (16PF)™ (adapted from Conn and Rieke, 1994)	• Perfectionism: degree to which an individual is motivated to be precise and correct. • Openness to change: comfort with emerging, uncertain situations. • Apprehension: degree to which an individual is a worrier, doubt-filled and lacking in confidence. • Rule Consciousness: tendency to be conformist and traditional rather than pushing the boundaries of what is perceived to be expected by others.
Marston's DISC model™ (Dominance, Influence, Steadiness, Compliance) (Marston, 2007)	• Assertive or passive behavioural preferences. • Open or guarded behavioural preferences. • Dominance and Influence tend to lead to more risk-taking preferences, whereas Steadiness and Compliance are associated with caution.

to gain insight into how they might naturally behave if they followed only their instincts when making decisions. There is certainly no single, reliable diagnostic that can be used to determine the risk preferences or propensity of individual decision-makers; indeed the fact that these constructs are internal tendencies should warn us against trying to be overly analytical about them.

In addition to personality profiles that have arisen largely as management tools, academics interested in the decision sciences also have things to say about 'measuring' risk preferences. Some decision scientists argue that risk-taking is a rational, economic process, where human beings are able to compute potential gains and losses and decide objectively (for example, Dyer and Sarin, 1982; Davies, 2006). Others argue that there are other, more subjective, situational influences on risk propensity (for example, Sitkin and Pablo, 1992; Lopes, 1987; Sitkin and Weingart, 1995). In our view, based on our own experience with risky decision-making, we rarely see people behaving as dispassionate rational economic actors.

Measuring group risk culture. Risk preferences and risk propensity apply to individuals, yet individuals rarely make decisions in a vacuum. Individuals form decision-making groups such as families, project teams, company boards, and so on. Groups, particularly long-established ones such as companies, will tend to adopt tendencies of how to respond to risk and this collective tendency is referred to as the group's risk culture. For example, one organisation's risk culture might be always to consider how to avoid any loss that might be associated with risk, while another might view risk as an opportunity to maximise value.

By definition, culture is subjective and intangible. Although large-scale, respected studies have been undertaken to try to identify features of national and organisational cultures, the work on risk culture is far less well developed, as documented in the recent two reports from the Institute of Risk Management (2012).

A number of major consultancies have risk cultural diagnostic processes as part of their offering, and these tend to build a qualitative picture, based on data from interviews and surveys of the behaviours of managers in firms that shape and define the culture for risk-taking. Aspects of culture 'measured' by these processes include:

- The degree of challenge, openness and confidence displayed

- The degree of tolerance for alternative views, transparency of communication and level of insight displayed

- The degree to which cooperation and respect for rules exists

- The speed of response and levels of care in responding that can be observed.

Analysis of an organisation using such an approach can identify strengths and weaknesses in the ability to deal with risk, but they cannot 'measure' risk culture directly. Other approaches are more simplistic, attempting to fit risk cultures into a 2×2 matrix, and these are less useful.

In the academic rather than practitioner literature, some diagnostics exist that attempt to measure risk culture, although even in the better diagnostics, the term risk culture is often used interchangeably with risk attitude, incorrectly in our view (for example, Underwood and Ingram, 2010).

In summary, individual risk preferences, individual risk propensity and organisational risk culture are important influential factors when considering risk appetite, but they are not directly observable and measurable. Instead they are internal tendencies that can be assessed to some degree through the use of diagnostics at an individual or group level. Rather than trying to measure these tendencies per se, it is more important to consider how each may be affecting risk appetite and the resulting risk thresholds. Instruments for diagnosing aspects of risk preferences or risk culture are therefore only of limited use insofar as they help individuals and groups to reflect on their internal tendencies.

THE INFORMED SCENARIO: FACTORS UNDERSTOOD AND CONTROLLED WITH HINDSIGHT

In the Informed Scenario, the externally measurable factors in the RARA Model that were determined in the Constrained Scenario are supplemented by an understanding of the factors that influence risk attitude, as shown in Figure 6.4.

Although diagnostics exist that seek to evaluate the tendencies to take risk at individual and group level (risk preferences and risk culture), these measures have use only insofar that they can alert the decision-maker to what is likely to happen. In the Informed Scenario, by contrast, the mediating factor of risk attitude is introduced. We define this term very precisely as a '*chosen response* to a given risky situation, influenced by perception'. Crucially, risk attitude is a situational phenomenon. It cannot be measured directly, but it can be understood and judged as appropriate or inappropriate during decision-making in a specific risky and important situation.

Although risk attitude is a chosen response, the things that influence risk attitude are mostly not chosen. These need to be explored and understood to enable that chosen response to be made and upheld.

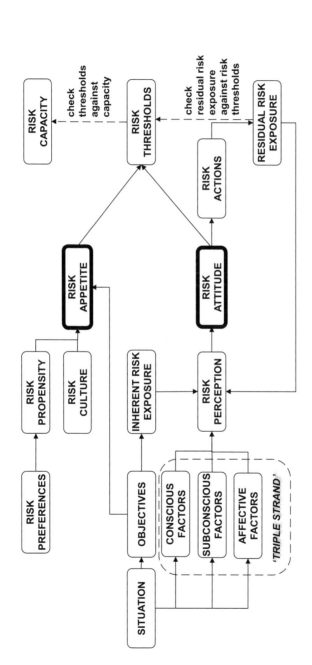

Figure 6.4   Influences on risk thresholds in the Informed Scenario

Risk attitude is influenced by risk perception which in turn is influenced by the inherent risk exposure in the situation (which can be objectively determined) and the 'triple strand' of conscious, subconscious and affective influences shown in the dotted box in the RARA Model and shown here as Figure 6.5.

CONSCIOUS FACTORS (rational assessments)

SUBCONSCIOUS FACTORS (heuristics and cognitive bias)

... together influence perception and risk attitude

AFFECTIVE FACTORS (feelings and emotions)

Figure 6.5 **The Triple Strand of influences on perception and risk attitude (reproduced from Murray-Webster and Hillson, 2008, used with permission)**

Conscious, subconscious and affective factors can all be reflected upon and understood, either in isolation, or, more importantly, as a combined effect. Many things influence our attitudes to risks, because many things influence our perception of whether a situation is risky or not and to what extent. Some of the factors are situational and can be rationally analysed, such as past experience, or closeness of the risk in time. Others are based on feelings and emotions such as fear, worry or joy, and these are called affective factors. Situational and affective factors are obviously personal: each individual will be influenced differently.

Research shows that a third set of influences work subconsciously and tend to influence people similarly. These subconscious influences are usually referred to as cognitive biases (factors that skew how we perceive and think about things). Others are mental short-cuts (heuristics) that allow us to process information quickly, but sometimes erroneously. You may have heard people speak of optimism bias – this is an example of a cognitive bias that seems to have a systematic effect on our ability to estimate under uncertainty (Flyvbjerg, 2008). You may also have heard of the availability heuristic (most recent or most memorable information has undue influence), or the anchoring heuristic (where we become irrationally influenced by the idea first suggested to us) (Slovic, 2000; Tversky and Kahnemann, 1974).

The significance of the 'triple strand' is that although there are many factors that influence our perception of a risky situation, at the point of perception they are all tightly intertwined and it is difficult to unravel them. Our argument is that if people are to understand their risk attitudes in making particularly risky and important decisions, so that they can manage those risk attitudes proactively and intentionally, then they need to be able to unpick the strands and get to the root causes of the influences on perception. For individuals, much can be achieved through reflection, perhaps supported by discussion with colleagues or a coach.

If the 'triple strand' applies to individuals, does it also apply to decision-making groups, such as boards, investment committees, steering groups, project boards, and so on? In our view it does. Of course, each individual in the decision-making group will have their own influences, but there are also group effects. You may well have heard of group cognitive biases such as groupthink

(Janis, 1971). In organisational life, the term groupthink is used widely, almost as part of our everyday understanding of the potential for group dynamics to influence decision-making. It tends to be used loosely to describe situations when decision-makers feel there is 'safety in numbers' and where groups end up making a decision that none of the individual members of the group would have made alone. Irving Janis, the social psychologist who pioneered the work on this phenomenon, is clear that groups of people working together are subject to powerful social pressures to conform with the norms of the particular group. He would argue that social conformity and group morale are more important than critical thinking when key decisions are to be made.

So in decision-making groups there is an even more complex cocktail of influences, including both those that affect each individual member of the group, as well as collective biases that are a feature of the group dynamics.

Although the influences on risk perception, and therefore risk attitude are complex and intertwined, it is nevertheless possible to choose a risk attitude in a particular situation.

The language that has been commonly adopted to describe risk attitudes is shown below in Table 6.2.

We have frequently seen and heard practitioners mix up the language and apply these labels to risk appetite rather than risk attitude. We argue this is wrong because risk appetite is an internal tendency and not a choice. Using the example of the size of beef steak again, if my appetite is for a 600-gram/ 20-ounce T-bone, then that is a fact. If the risks in the situation lead me to conclude that a T-bone may not be available, then I can choose my risk attitude to suit that situation. I might be

Table 6.2 **Definition of risk attitudes (reproduced from Murray-Webster and Hillson, 2008, used with permission)**

Term	Definition
Risk-averse	Uncomfortable with uncertainty, desire to avoid or reduce threats and exploit opportunities to remove uncertainty. Would be unhappy with an uncertain outcome.
Risk-seeking	Comfortable with uncertainty, no desire to avoid or reduce threats or to exploit opportunities to remove uncertainty. Would be happy with an uncertain outcome.
Risk-tolerant	Tolerant of uncertainty, no strong desire to respond to threats or opportunities in any way. Could tolerate an uncertain outcome if necessary.
Risk-neutral	Uncomfortable with uncertainty in the long term so prepared to take whatever short-term actions are necessary to deliver a certain long-term outcome.

very uncomfortable with the situation (risk-averse) and choose to be very proactive to ensure that the risks are dealt with in a manner as to give me the best chance of satisfying my appetite (decide now to order ribs, for example). I could choose, however, to be more relaxed and tolerate the risks, being prepared to have the 400-gram/12-ounce sirloin (maybe with some extra vegetables) if the T-bone was not available. I could also choose to take a chance that something else good and filling will be available for dinner (risk-seeking).

This simplistic example illustrates a key point for decision-making in risky and important situations: it is vital to find a way of aligning chosen risk attitudes with the risk appetite of the organisation, expressed by risk thresholds. Application of the RARA Model enables that alignment.

If we extend the eating example to common work examples, we can illustrate further how dealing with risky situations requires adaptation of risk attitude to enable residual risk to fit within thresholds that reflect the risk appetite.

In business, it is common for risk thresholds to be articulated by defining probability and impact scales on a risk assessment matrix or heat map. Such techniques make it clear how much risk would be too much to tolerate when thinking about single, discrete risks. If the combined probability and size of impact of the risk falls above the most risky threshold, it is often assumed that the chosen risk attitude of responsible managers would be risk-averse, a discomfort with the exposure that resulted in a drive to manage the risk to reduce exposure. Of course, this is a risky assumption and a common error in organisations is not to make more effort to ensure that risk attitude is aligned with risk appetite.

CHOOSE A RISK ATTITUDE THAT FITS WITH THE RISK APPETITE

Given that we argue that the single point of control in the RARA Model is the chosen risk attitude of the decision-makers, how can we make the final step in the process and demonstrate how chosen risk attitude can be evaluated and modified in a specific situation? This can be done using the Six 'A's Model (Murray-Webster and Hillson, 2008), shown in Figure 6.6.

The Six 'A's model provides a structured framework to help individuals and groups adopt an appropriate risk attitude in any given risky and important situation. The model is

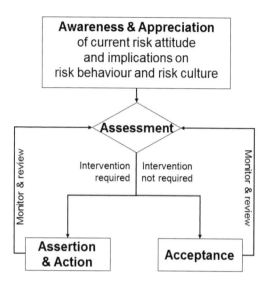

Figure 6.6   The Six 'A's' Model (based on Murray-Webster and Hillson, 2008, used with permission)

described in detail elsewhere (Murray-Webster and Hillson, 2008), but it can be summarised as follows:

- First, there is a need for *Awareness* and *Appreciation* of the current risk attitude adopted by an individual or a group, including the 'triple strand' key influences.

- Next comes *Assessment*, to determine whether the unmanaged risk attitude is likely to lead to an acceptable outcome or not.

- Where the assessment step indicates that intervention is required to modify the prevailing risk attitude, *Assertion* and *Action* are employed to make the necessary change.

- If on the other hand assessment shows that the existing risk attitude is appropriate, the current risk attitude can be *Accepted*.

- Whether the unmanaged risk attitude is accepted or modified, the ongoing situation must be monitored and reassessed periodically to determine whether intervention may be required at a later time.

Each of these steps involves a range of underlying actions. We have shown how 'chosen risk attitude' works alongside the other risk-related elements of the RARA Model to provide a control loop that can be activated to modify risk attitude where necessary, influencing both the level at which risk thresholds are set and the nature of future risk actions. Since risk appetite is an internal and independent tendency not influenced by human choice, it cannot act in this modifying way, leaving our ability to choose an appropriate risk attitude as the sole control point available to us.

SUMMARY: WHAT CAN WE MEASURE?

As we have seen, some risk-related factors exist independently outside people and in the external environment, and hence these can be observed and/or measured. These form the starting point when considering how much risk is too much risk: the elements of the Unmanaged Scenario. The other risk-related factors that allow the Unmanaged Scenario to progress through to an informed judgement are intangible and they cannot be measured directly; they can only be observed through actions or proxy measures.

We argue that the control point in the process is achieved by comparing the objective expression of risk thresholds with the evaluation of residual risk, and modifying risk attitude as necessary to ensure that residual risk is matched with thresholds so that the situation poses neither too much nor too little risk.

Risk-related concepts, by their nature, are difficult to articulate and measure given that risk relates to the future, not the past. In this chapter we have used the classification of the risk-related factors in the RARA Model shown in Figure 6.1 to contrast which elements are external to people and which are internal. Also we have shown which elements are independent of human choice, and those where an explicit choice can be made to modify behaviour and provide a point of control in a complex system.

Now we have fully explained the RARA Model in principle, and related it to practical examples (in Chapter 5) and other existing expressions and 'measures' of behaviour in risky situations (in Chapter 6), we have everything we need to outline a simple step-by-step approach that can be applied to move through the three scenarios and come up with 'an answer' to the key risk question: 'How much risk would it be appropriate for you to take in a particular situation given all the influencing factors?'

REFERENCES

Briggs-Myers, I. and Myers, P.B. 1980. *Gifts Differing: Understanding Personality Type.* California, USA: Consulting Psychology Practice.

Conn, S.R., and Rieke, M.L. 1994. *The 16PF Fifth Edition Technical Manual.* Champagne IL, USA: Institute for Personality and Ability Testing, Inc.

Davies, G.B. 2006. 'Rethinking risk attitude: Aspiration as pure risk'. *Theory and Decision*, 61 (2), 159–90.

Dyer, J.S. and Sarin, R.K. 1982. 'Relative risk aversion'. *Management Science*, 28 (8), 875–86.

Flyvbjerg, B. 2008. 'Curbing optimism bias and strategic misrepresentation in planning: Reference class forecasting in practice'. *European Planning Studies*, 16 (1), 3–21.

Institute of Risk Management. 2012. *Risk Culture: Resources for Practitioners*. London, UK: Institute of Risk Management.

Institute of Risk Management. 2012. *Risk Culture Under the Microscope: Guidance for Boards*. London, UK: Institute of Risk Management.

Janis, I. 1971. 'Groupthink'. *Psychology Today*, November 1971, 43.

Lopes, L.L. 1987. 'Between hope and fear: The psychology of risk'. *Advances in Experimental Social Psychology*, 20, 255–95.

Marston, W. M. 2007. *Emotions of Normal People*. (first published 1928). London, UK: Read Books.

Murray-Webster, R. and Hillson, D.A. 2008. *Managing Group Risk Attitude*. Aldershot, UK: Gower.

Sitkin, S.B. and Pablo, A. 1992. 'Reconceptualising the determinants of risk behaviour'. *Academy of Management Review*, 17 (1), 9–38.

Sitkin, S.B. and Weingart, L.R. 1995. 'Determinants of risk decision-making behaviour: A test of the mediating role of risk perception and risk propensity'. *Academy of Management Journal*, 38 (6), 1573–92.

Slovic, P. 2000. *Perception of Risk*. London, UK: Earthscan Press.

Spony G. 2003. 'The development of a work-value model assessing the cumulative impact of individual and cultural differences on managers' work-value systems'. *International Journal of Human Resource Management*, 14 (4), 658–79.

Sugerman, J., Scullard, M. and Wilhelm, E. 2011. *The 8 Dimensions of Leadership: DISC Strategies for Becoming a Better Leader*. Minneapolis MN, USA: Inscape Publishing Inc.

Trickey, G. and Stewart, M. 2010. *The Risk-Type Compass Manual*. Tunbridge Wells, UK: Psychological Consultancy Ltd.

Tversky, A. and Kahnemann, D. 1974. 'Judgement under uncertainty: Heuristics and biases', *Science*, 211, 453–8.

Underwood, A. and Ingram, D. 2010. 'The full spectrum of risk attitude'. *The Actuary*, 7 (4) 26–32.

(7) Using the RARA Model in Practice

In Chapters 3 and 4 we looked at various risk terms relating to the question 'How much risk will we take?' Starting with the two main concepts of risk appetite and risk attitude, we built up a detailed description of how the different factors interact, resulting in an overall framework which we call the RARA Model because of the central roles played by risk appetite and risk attitude (see Figure 4.3).

We also discovered in Chapter 4 that it is not possible to express or measure risk appetite directly, because it is an internal and invisible tendency within individuals and groups. Instead we need to use an external measurable proxy that is derived from risk appetite, and that role is played by risk thresholds. So when managers and decision-makers try to answer the 'How much risk … ' questions, the outcome can only be expressed through the risk thresholds that they set.

We then progressively deconstructed the full RARA Model in Chapter 5 to show the effect that both risk appetite and risk attitude have on setting risk thresholds, describing three scenarios which demonstrate the effect of incrementally adding first risk appetite and then risk attitude. And in Chapter 6 we expanded those three scenarios by exploring which of the risk-related factors can be measured directly and which cannot.

Now we are ready to offer practical guidelines on how management teams can use the RARA Model to understand and express their risk appetite through setting appropriate risk thresholds, in order to support better risk-informed decision-making. We can use the three scenarios from Chapter 5 as a framework for developing a simple stepwise process. As a reminder, these are the three scenarios we described earlier:

1. **Unmanaged**, where risk thresholds are set by the organisation with no conscious or intentional reference to risk appetite or risk attitude (see Figure 5.1 and Figure 6.2).

2. **Constrained**, where risk thresholds are consciously modified by an understanding of the inherent risk appetite (Figure 5.2 and Figure 6.3).

3. **Informed**, taking account of the chosen risk attitudes of key stakeholders as well as wider organisational factors when setting risk thresholds (Figure 5.3 and Figure 6.4).

Our suggested process moves through these three scenarios in turn, starting with the outcome arising from the Unmanaged Scenario of the RARA Model, then adding in the effect of risk appetite via the Constrained Scenario, and finally using the control provided by chosen risk attitude as described in the Informed Scenario. This process starts by taking account of external and visible factors to generate an initial set of risk thresholds, without conscious consideration of the hidden influences (the Unmanaged Scenario). This is then augmented and modified by taking account of the pre-existing tendencies of individuals and the organisation in relation to risk (risk propensities and risk culture), which produces an intangible risk appetite that modifies the first-cut risk thresholds and allows them to be compared with the organisation's risk capacity (the Constrained Scenario). Finally a further refinement of risk thresholds is achieved (if necessary) through active adoption of the desirable risk attitude in order to optimise the achievement of objectives given the level of risk exposure (the Informed Scenario).

Why is this stepwise process necessary? Why can we not simply state how much risk we are prepared to take in a given situation, without having to consider the various risk-related factors in the RARA Model?

Clearly it is not safe to rely on the Unmanaged Scenario, since this produces risk thresholds based on gut reaction and intuition, taking no account of the organisational risk culture or the risk propensities of key stakeholders. As a minimum we need to consider the norms of 'the way we do things here' and 'how much risk the organisation (or part of the organisation) can bear' as produced by the Constrained Scenario. But we have shown that even this is not sufficient to ensure that risk thresholds are set in an appropriate place. Instead we need to actively adopt a risk attitude that reflects our chosen response to the perceived risk exposure, which will in turn influence where we decide to set our risk thresholds, as shown in the Informed Scenario.

MOVING THROUGH THE SCENARIOS

In order to make this process explicit, we recommend that risk thresholds should be set in a progressive manner, moving through the three scenarios in four distinct steps, with an intermediate check. These four steps are described in the following paragraphs and illustrated in Figure 7.1.

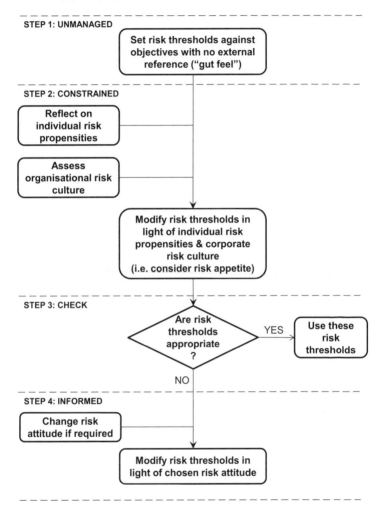

Figure 7.1   Setting risk thresholds using risk appetite and risk attitude

Step 1: Unmanaged. The first step is for decision-makers to produce and record risk thresholds without reference to any factors other than what can be described and measured. This can be done in a facilitated workshop with the key stakeholders, where they are encouraged to express their personal perspective on how much risk can be taken in the given situation, measured in the same units as the agreed objectives.

The facilitator is effectively asking them to express their 'gut feel' for how much risk can be taken, with no criticism or qualification, and no need to explain the reasons behind their views. Of course each individual decision-maker will be influenced by their inherent risk appetite, but this is not made explicit at this stage, and so the effects of risk appetite remain unseen. The key challenge for the facilitator in this situation is to help the decision-making group to reach consensus on risk thresholds, which might be difficult when the factors influencing their gut feel are not openly visible.

Step 2: Constrained. The initial risk thresholds recorded in Step 1 are then modified to take account of the risk appetite of the organisation and key stakeholders. In this step the decision-makers are explicitly asked to reflect on two factors:

● The risk propensities of key stakeholders

● The underlying organisational risk culture.

Again the support of an experienced and skilled facilitator can be vital in helping them to understand what is influencing their inherent risk appetite, using various techniques such as visualisation or appreciative inquiry. Each individual can be encouraged to reflect on their personal risk propensity and underlying risk preferences, using a range of approaches drawn from the fields of emotional literacy and psychometrics. The decision-making group should also consider the prevailing corporate risk culture, to determine the extent to which it encourages risk-taking or risk-averse behaviour.

Having thought about their individual risk propensities and the organisational risk culture, and the effect these have on the level of risk that can be taken in the given situation, the initial risk thresholds should then be adjusted to take explicit account of these influences. In effect this step produces modified risk thresholds that take account of the current risk appetite, since risk appetite is driven by both individual risk propensities and organisational risk culture.

Step 3: Check. The risk thresholds defined through this route then need to be validated to determine whether they are appropriate. This validation has two elements. The first part is to compare the risk thresholds with the risk capacity. Although this checking forms part of the Constrained Scenario (as described in Chapter 5), we recommend that it is done as a separate step in order to highlight its importance. In most cases this can't be done in isolation from risk thresholds for other situations, since the risk thresholds for this particular situation will need to be considered as part of the overall risk exposure that the organisation is carrying. In other words it would be very unlikely for the risk thresholds set for an individual project to exceed the overall risk capacity of the wider organisation. Instead the project risk thresholds need to be assessed within the portfolio of other projects and related activities, to determine whether in aggregate the organisational risk capacity might be exceeded.

But secondly we need to consider whether the risk thresholds that have emerged from the Constrained step will help us to achieve our chosen objectives within the given risky situation. This is where we answer the question 'Are we taking too much risk – or too little?'

If these two checks indicate that the risk thresholds we have set are appropriate, then we can go ahead and use them within our overall risk management approach. But if we feel that the risk thresholds are not right, then we need to make a conscious and intentional change to them. This takes us to the final step in our process.

Step 4: Informed. A final refinement to the risk thresholds from Step 2 can be made if necessary, by choosing a different risk attitude to help us modify the decision on how much risk to take in the given situation. We have already highlighted the key role of risk attitude in the RARA Model as a control point in the process of setting risk thresholds, since this is where individuals and groups can intentionally choose a different risk attitude.

As we discussed in Chapter 6, the Six 'A's model (Figure 6.6) provides a practical approach to facilitate the appropriate choice of risk attitude. Working through the Six 'A's, the decision-making group can first seek to understand the current risk attitude that exists when they consider the situation at hand (Awareness and Appreciation). With the help of the facilitator they then Assess whether this risk attitude, in combination with the inherent risk appetite, is producing an appropriate outcome in terms of decisions about risk thresholds. If there is no need to change then the current risk attitude can be Accepted, but if it is necessary to intervene then the group needs to Assert the need for change and take the required Actions to adopt a new risk attitude. This new risk attitude can then be used to inform the decision about risk thresholds, as the participants actively decide to modify risk thresholds in the light of their newly chosen risk attitude.

MULTI-LEVEL RISK APPETITE

The only other matter to consider is how the risk thresholds for any particular set of objectives might fit as part of a wider set of objectives and thresholds. As we explored in our discussion of the examples in Chapter 5, the factors that influence inherent risk appetite and chosen risk attitude are most likely to be different at different levels of the organisation, as they are mostly driven by the characteristics of the people involved. But these factors all exist at multiple levels within an organisation.

This is illustrated by the four types of example decisions that we discussed in Chapter 5, which we called My Decision (a personal choice made by an individual), the Operational Decision (made by a manager within part of an organisation), the Strategic Decision (determining the overall direction to take), and the Community Decision (where objectives are not commercial but they affect a lot of people). There are clear differences in these situations, though they are all risky and important.

The need to set risk thresholds within a hierarchy is also clear when we consider the position of projects. A number of stakeholders must be able to answer the 'How much risk … ' question for a particular project, including the project sponsor, the project team, and the ultimate client. But an individual project does not exist in isolation – it usually sits within a programme or a portfolio of projects and other activities. And the benefits produced from the portfolio will contribute to a department or business unit, which in turn forms part of the performance of the overall organisation. In a mature organisation, risk appetites will be considered and risk thresholds will be set at each of these levels: project, programme/portfolio, department and organisational. But these risk thresholds must be coherent and aligned if the organisation is to function effectively. If lower-level thresholds are not set with conscious and deliberate reference to the risk appetite of higher levels, then problems are inevitable.

So how can a project sponsor know how much risk is acceptable on his project if risk thresholds have not been explicitly set for the programme within which this project sits? Conversely the departmental head cannot determine whether the activities within her business unit are exceeding her risk threshold without a clear steer on what levels of risk exposure will be deemed acceptable by the board.

We have explained in this chapter how to set appropriate risk thresholds in a single isolated setting, such as a defined decision that is both risky and important. But when that decision exists in a wider context, we need to take that into account. How?

In the four-step process we have described (Figure 7.1), the context is considered in Step 3 Check. Here the risk thresholds that have emerged from the first two steps in the process are compared with risk capacity, to indicate whether we can move forward using these risk thresholds, or whether they may need to be modified. Like risk thresholds, risk capacity is described using the same units as our objectives, for example time delay, cost over-run, variation in share-price or market share, and so on. So when we are checking our risk thresholds against risk capacity, we are comparing like with like. But we need to aggregate lower-level risk thresholds when comparing them with higher levels of risk capacity.

The most practical way of dealing with this is for the decision-maker(s) to explicitly understand their objectives and the associated risk thresholds in the context of both higher level objectives/risk thresholds and those at a lower level. A classic example would be in a programme scenario where the programme objectives need to be understood in the context of both wider business objectives and also subordinate project objectives. The same would apply to a business unit within an operation that reported into a higher level group, but also was responsible for subunits, such as a manufacturing plant, a bank branch or an individual high-street store.

This treatment of the wider context is most commonly seen when risk thresholds are used to define escalation or delegation criteria, determining when lower-level risks should be reported upwards for attention or action, or conversely when risks identified at a higher level need to be passed further down the organisation to be managed. These escalation/delegation criteria effectively quantify the risk capacity within which each part of the organisation must manage. We can only deal with multiple levels of risk appetite properly if these criteria and boundaries are agreed and clearly communicated to all concerned.

'HOW MUCH RISK WILL WE TAKE?': THE ANSWER

The simple stepwise process outlined in this chapter allows people who have to make a risky and important decision to do so in a way that takes proper account of all of the important factors. The end result is a set of risk thresholds defined against each objective, which properly reflect the inherent risk appetite of key stakeholders and the organisation, but which have been modified intentionally and intelligently by the choice of an appropriate risk attitude to produce the optimal outcome.

By following these four steps, organisations can be confident that they are setting risk thresholds which meet the corporate governance requirements of regulators to define and express their risk appetite. But they can also be sure that those risk thresholds meet the needs of the business, while at the same time taking full account of individual risk propensities and corporate risk culture. At the end of the day they will finally have succeeded in setting risk thresholds that answer the key question with which we started: 'How much risk will we take?'

⑧ Conclusions

In this book we've explained that understanding risk appetite is a key part of decision-making and we've shown how risk appetite is linked to other risk-related terms through our RARA Model. In this final chapter, we summarise the business case for applying the RARA Model in practice. Why should you use it?

BUSINESS CASE FOR THE RARA MODEL

Research on risk appetite carried out in 2009 by the Association of Insurance and Risk Managers (AIRMIC) identified four ways in which organisations can benefit from understanding and expressing their risk appetite. They outline the role of risk appetite in *supporting strategy-setting*, leading to a balanced risk profile and identification of which risks to avoid and which to take at a strategic level. They suggest that risk appetite supports *setting appropriate boundaries for risk-taking* so that decision-makers are able to make better and more consistent decisions. AIRMIC argue that understanding risk appetite helps organisations understand what risk management resources they need and how to allocate them to foster a risk-aware culture and to *support effective management of risk.* Finally they make the point that effective risk management enhances organisational performance and delivery, and therefore *maximises stakeholder value.*

COSO's *Enterprise Risk Management – Integrated Framework* (2004) introduced the idea of risk appetite, and their view was expanded and explained in their 2012 report *Enterprise Risk Management – Understanding and Communicating Risk Appetite.* COSO's position is similar to AIRMIC in pointing out that risk appetite statements are needed to guide and align strategy-setting and resource-allocation, to align the organisation to take the right amount of risk, and to reflect the organisation's philosophy, style and culture towards risk. They put definitions of risk appetite at the start of a commitment to Enterprise Risk Management, in order to secure tangible organisational value.

Our argument on why risk appetite is important is constructed slightly differently.

All decisions are made in the face of uncertainties that would matter if they occurred. In such risky and important decisions, some people might try to eliminate risk, even though this is both unachievable and undesirable. This is partly because risk includes both threats and opportunities, so trying to remove downside risk (threats) might also reduce upside risk (opportunities). But it also makes no economic sense to try to make an uncertain world certain. Not only would we fail, but we would waste scarce resources trying.

The other extreme is to ignore risk and 'take your chance', or to understand risk but do nothing about it. We argue that this course of action is irresponsible, failing to exercise a duty of care to stakeholders and shareholders, and not taking proper account of the impact of risk on the world, its resources, or current and future generations.

So if ignoring risk is irresponsible, and trying to eliminate risk is futile and wasteful, the middle ground must be to decide 'How much risk would be too much risk' to take in a situation, and then to put in place mechanisms and controls to ensure that you stay on track as time passes.

Some believe that merely understanding our risk appetite will be enough to allow us to manage risk effectively. Others rely on implementing robust risk processes or tools. Another group think that understanding and managing risk attitude is the key. Our view is that each of these only offers a partial solution, and on their own they are of dubious value.

The business case for risk management only makes sense if all aspects are brought together, and this is what the RARA Model does. We have taken you on a journey from the confusion of multiple risk-related terms in Chapter 3, through to developing the RARA Model in Chapter 4, then we've detailed how to apply the model and measure various elements in Chapters 5 and 6, with a simple application flowchart in Chapter 7.

When you look at the large volume of work from regulatory bodies, standards organisations, professional associations and consultants as outlined in Chapter 2, you might think that creating organisational value from risk appetite would be easy. But it's not easy because so much of the published information is conflicting. Our work cuts through the confusion and comprehensively defines the range of risk-related terms, explaining how these relate to the questions at the heart of risky decision-making.

HOW MUCH RISK WILL WE TAKE? AND OTHER RISKY QUESTIONS

Although this book is about risk appetite, we have shown how it is impossible to know how much risk to take without considering a set of other questions that are important when taking management decisions. These other questions relate to different but related risk concepts, including the following:

- How much risk do we usually like to take? [risk propensity /risk culture]

- How much risk do we want to take? [risk appetite]

- How much risk can we take? [risk capacity]

- How much risk do we think we are taking? [risk perception]

- How much risk do we think we should take? [risk attitude]

- How much risk are we taking? [risk exposure]

Each of these questions is important and some can be answered in isolation. For example, it is normal for many organisations to determine their overall risk exposure, which is a measure of the overall effect of identified risks on objectives. Our main argument, however, is that, to make the best decisions in risky situations, it is necessary to answer all the questions and consolidate those 'answers' into objective and measurable risk thresholds for each objective. Risk thresholds then define the target variability levels for objectives, guiding the choice of risk attitude to be adopted, and shaping the risk actions that follow.

In fact it is risk thresholds that finally articulate the answer to the key question, 'How much risk will we take?'

Our recent consulting work has made it clear that if organisations don't follow this approach, then their rationale and business case for investing in risk management is invalidated. Without understanding their risk appetite, expressing this via risk thresholds and choosing appropriate risk attitudes, people in an organisation may identify risks to objectives, but they have no mechanism for knowing how much risk can be borne, or how much risk senior decision-makers or shareholders are prepared to bear. This disconnect continues as people invest scarce resources in trying to reduce risk and uncertainty, but without having a sound business case for the investment. The situation is further compounded when individuals and teams have no mechanism in place for dealing with differences in perception of what is risky and why, and no understanding of attitudes to risk-taking – all of which complicates and confuses any rational analysis.

Risk management is too important a topic to be left to chance! As a result, our work to systematically define risk-related terms and join them into a single framework (the RARA Model) provides a practical approach that individuals and teams can use to ensure that they take the right risks safely. Within the RARA Model, risk appetite and risk attitude have central and complementary roles. It is our hope that this book will help practitioners to cut through the extensive and conflicting data that is already 'out there'. In doing so, they can help themselves, their employers, their communities and their families to make good decisions in risky and important situations.

REFERENCES

Association of Insurance and Risk Managers. 2009. *Research into the Definition and Application of the Concept of Risk Appetite.* London, UK: Association of Insurance and Risk Managers (AIRMIC).

Committee of Sponsoring Organizations of the Treadway Commission (COSO). 2004. *Enterprise Risk Management – Integrated Framework.* New York NY, USA: AICPA.

Committee of Sponsoring Organizations of the Treadway Commission (COSO). 2012. *Enterprise Risk Management – Understanding and Communicating Risk Appetite.* Available at http://www.coso.org/documents/ERM-Understanding%20 %20Communicating%20Risk%20Appetite-WEB_FINAL_ r9.pdf. Accessed 18 August 2012.

Index

Reviews of the *Short Guides to Risk* Series

Procurement Risk

'I'm genuinely amazed at the breadth of risks that this little book covers...In this Guide Richard describes the journey to build good procurement risk management; what is at stake, how to describe and address it. He goes further to show how to build commitment across the wider business cross-functional team, raising the profile of the procurement process and know-how, shaping and developing expertise that actually builds collaborative working in the business. These are critical and highly valuable goals for every Senior Leader seeking to deliver sustainable value and high performing teams.'
– Paula Gildert, Head of Development Strategic Sourcing, Novartis Pharmaceuticals, Switzerland.

Fraud Risk

'Superfunds readers would be familiar with the talents and writing skills of the authors...A Short Guide to Fraud Risk is an ideal introduction to the subject in easily accessible language... Each chapter takes one part of the topic, puts it in context, gives examples and concludes with a brief summary of the key points...'
– Robert Hodge, ASFA's principal policy adviser and Superfunds technical editor

Ethical Risk

'Carlo does a wonderful job of relating ethics and risk to the global economy. Not only is he insightful, if we don't pay attention to the guidance described in this book individual companies will be at a significant risk and the global economy will suffer.'
– Roy Snell CCEP-Fellow, Chief Executive Officer, Society of Corporate Compliance and Ethics

Customs Risk

'I have now been for almost three years an excise and systems director at Malta Customs, and Catherine Truel's book is really serving me as my first practical point of reference on customs risk and related areas. It is certainly invaluable for the handy small size of the book and I would undoubtedly recommend it to anyone involved in or studying international trade policy and administrative matters.'
– Martin E Spiteri, Director Excise and Systems, Ministry of Finance, the Economy and Investment, Malta

A Short Guide to Facilitating Risk Management

'The book provides a clear introduction to tackling risk (including opportunities) in a fun, professional way, with the aim of gaining consensus. It's pragmatic and practical, with real-life examples to show how risk management can become ingrained in the day-to-day management of initiatives in your organisation.'
– Elizabeth Harrin, author of *Project Management in the Real World* and Head of IT Programme Delivery, Spire Healthcare

'The book makes a compelling case for the role of a risk management facilitator, to ease the operation of risk management processes by enthusing and engaging people, and by maintaining continued ownership and accountability until the risks have been closed.'
– John Greenwood

Other titles from Gower by
David Hillson and Ruth Murray-Webster

A Short Guide to Facilitating Risk Management
Penny Pullan and Ruth Murray-Webster
Paperback: 978-1-4094-0730-0

Exploiting Future Uncertainty
David Hillson
Paperback: 978-1-4094-2341-6

Managing Group Risk Attitude
Ruth Murray-Webster and David Hillson
Hardback: 978-0-566-08787-5

Managing Risk in Projects
David Hillson, Risk Doctor & Partners, UK
Paperback: 978-0-566-08867-4

Understanding and Managing Risk Attitude
David Hillson and Ruth Murray-Webster
Paperback: 978-0-566-08798-1

Vist the authors' page on our website:
http://www.ashgate.com/default.aspx?page=3224

GOWER